Shermin,

Thank y[illegible]s journey [illegible] me. I hope you will be inspired by the MisBehaving women who inspired my own journey. As you're reading their about their journey, allow their stories to enter your heart and touch your soul.

Forever & Always

MISBEHAVE

Speak Truth to Power

Dawn Nicole Martin

INKWATER PRESS

PORTLAND • OREGON

INKWATERPRESS.COM

Cover design: Niki Blaker
Cover layout and interior design by Masha Shubin
"Suffragettes on way to Boston" Bain Collection. Library of Congress.

Library of Congress Control Number: 2011927366

Publisher: Inkwater Press | www.inkwaterpress.com

Hardback
ISBN-13 978-1-59299-581-3 | ISBN-10 1-59299-581-0

Paperback
ISBN-13 978-1-59299-582-0 | ISBN-10 1-59299-582-9

Kindle
ISBN-13 978-1-59299-583-7 | ISBN-10 1-59299-583-7

Printed in the U.S.A.
All paper is acid free and meets all ANSI standards for archival quality paper.

1 3 5 7 9 10 8 6 4 2

"... a great door for effective work has opened to me, and there are many who oppose me"

1 Corinthians 16:9

Contents

Acknowledgments

FIRST AND FOREMOST, I WOULD LIKE TO THANK GOD FOR HIS GRACE AND MERCY. For I am confident that the good work He began in me will continue until it's perfected.

To the greatest woman I know, my dear mother (mammy) who taught me that there is nothing wrong with being an individual and to always stand for what I believe in. I've been standing ever since.

To my one and only daughter, the true gem in my life. You possess the spirit and the fire of a great lineage of women. My prayer for you is to be successful in all that you do and always stay true to who you are. Always remember from whom your source and strength come.

To the other two gems in my life, my two wonderful sons. I pray that you will continue to be passionate about your goals and your dreams. Always being true to self and faithful to God.

Faye, you have supported me throughout every step of this journey. Many times the road was long and the journey rough; yet, you believed in my work and constantly encouraged and reminded me of my mission. In many ways, you have taught me to "MisBehave."

Thom Lemmons, thank you for your tireless devotion and commitment to this project. Without your expert guidance, this book would not be possible.

To all my biological sisters, sisters in Christ, sisters and "sistahs" in the struggle, I say thank you from the bottom of my heart. I thank God for each and every one of you. I am the woman I am today because of your grace, your wisdom, your strength, your many prayers and lots of advice. Your beauty will forever shine.

To all the women who are determined to pursue their dreams and rise above externally imposed limitations, this book is for you. I dare you to MisBehave: Speak Truth to Power.

About the Author

Dawn Nicole Martin was born in St. Joseph on the Caribbean island of Trinidad. After graduating from high school, she immigrated to the United States. A graduate of Caldwell College, Dawn is presently pursuing her master's degree at Villanova University.

She currently resides in suburban Maryland and enjoys her roles as mother, daughter, sister, friend, colleague, mentor, and confidante.

Dawn's work as a human resource consultant has made her an advocate for the humane and equitable treatment of everyone. She is especially interested in the empowerment of women on a mission to shatter glass ceilings throughout the country. With over fifteen years of HR and other professional services experience, Dawn has a proven track record of results and achievement at every level of career responsibility; she is known for her authentic and collaborative leadership style.

When not fighting the good fight for the empowerment of women, Dawn takes pleasure in gardening, enjoying nature in the woods and along the trails of her neighborhood, reading a good book, or watching a movie.

INTRODUCTION

"All My Life I Had to Fight"

THERE ARE CERTAIN DATES AND EVENTS IN OUR LIVES THAT CARRY PERMANENT personal significance—where the thoughts and memories stay with us forever. For some it's the birth of a baby; for others it may be a wedding anniversary; for still others the date may bring to mind a tragedy, or when a loved one was taken from this life. I will always remember that cold, crisp day in November.

That day started like any other ordinary day. As I brushed my teeth, I thought about the full schedule I had, which included two very important meetings with my superiors. One was a regularly scheduled one-on-one meeting to discuss projects, issues, progress on initiatives, and other routine matters. The other, however, would decide whether I would be promoted to vice president of my department, an advancement that had been promised if I fulfilled certain obligations.

That morning I also reflected on the events of the past week, running across my mind like a movie, and how painful and stressful work had become. The night before, for example, I had been at work late, splitting hairs with one of my superiors about the importance of having consistent policies for all employees and the message we would be sending if rank-and-file employees were held to different standards than managers and administrators. Another dispute playing out vividly in my head involved the seemingly endless struggle with our organization's corporate office as they finally completed their review of a compliance issue that could have put the organization at risk if knowingly left unaddressed. This issue had festered for months, and word had gotten out to some of our employees before the planned communication was ready—resulting in angry managers at my door who did not understand why we were making changes that would impact their employees. I did my best to defuse the tension, but the damage was done. I subsequently found out the source of the leak and took the employee to task on the importance of confidentiality and the problems created by releasing information other than through the proper channels. After a heated exchange, I was left to clean up the mess—as usual. Cleaning up messes at my organization seemed to be the rule and not the exception.

As I finished brushing my teeth and prepared to put on my makeup, I stared at myself in the mirror and did not recognize the person looking back at me: I had deep circles under my eyes and my face appeared thinner. It was clear that the stress was taking its toll on me. I looked through the window as the darkness gave way to light and I realized the trees in my backyard showed the brilliant yellows, oranges, and reds of autumn. I knew it was November because of the crisp morning air, but had failed to notice the beauty all around me.

As I finished getting dressed for work, the words from a Kirk Franklin song suddenly played in my head: "No matter what may come my way, my life is in your hands..."[1] It was as if the Holy Spirit was reassuring my soul that change was in the air and no matter what happened, I could rest assured that events were in the hands of God. By the end of that day, I would understand the significance of these words all too well. At that moment, I really had no idea what was in store or why the song had come into my mind.

After arriving at work, I was unable to log into my computer. I placed the necessary calls to the help desk and waited for someone to resolve my issue. This was frustrating, as I had a lot to do that morning and I needed to get into the system. Later that morning, however, I was able to log on without any problems, so I went through the day as planned until it was time for my first meeting.

Imagine my dismay when, during this meeting with my manager from corporate, I was told that I was being put on administrative leave. When I asked why, I received no clear reason. I was asked to leave my keys, my laptop, and my Blackberry, and to report to corporate the following Monday.

Shocked, I probed for answers, but I got none—at least, none that were anywhere near complete. My manager made some mention of the events earlier in the week involving the confrontation with the employee over the leaked information, and he also referred to the contents of an e-mail I had sent, questioning why corporate had sent an employee who had known attendance issues to another department at our local system. In the e-mail, I suggested that the employee probably should have been let go, but that our local system had become a dumping ground for employees who could not make it at corporate for one reason or another. The underperforming employee's presence in the department was never justified to me, but apparently, I was supposed to accept this decision without questioning it.

Having worked in human resources, I understood the significance of being on administrative leave: it was the calm before the storm. It is often used for disciplinary reasons or to permit an investigation that may lead to a termination. At the meeting, my manager never told me the exact reason for placing me on leave; he just kept saying that it would be explained to me the following Monday.

I thought about the events of the past week, and my heated discussion about the leak was the only issue that came to mind. Under usual HR policy such an event probably warranted a write-up, but not being placed on administrative leave. It dawned on me that this was a way to deny me the promotion I had been promised.

I also recalled several instances where I had challenged the status quo—perhaps I was being punished.

Struggling to control my emotions, I closed the door behind my supervisor as he left my office. I sat with my door closed as I decided whether or not I should call an attorney. I looked to the ceiling as if God might write an answer there, but no clear solutions came to me at that moment. I knew my superiors did not want me to air their dirty laundry. But if I decided to stay and fight, what type of toll would it take on my health?

And then, I could hear the Holy Spirit speaking to my soul again, and this time the message was, "This battle is not yours to fight." I came to a decision.

I immediately left my office to find my superior. As we spoke, I realized we both knew that my being put on leave was bullshit. I had been through this dance before with many employees and I knew what was next: I would be thanked for my service and given the canned speech about not being part of the organization, going forward. My manager kept saying that he was sorry all this was happening but that he still could not give me any answers.

A year earlier, during a period when the future of the organization was seriously in doubt, I was one of the employees who was asked to stay on and help "turn out the lights," as it were. I was told that in the near-miraculous event of the organization's continuance, I would receive a promotion to vice president—a promotion I had believed earlier in the day, ironically, that I was about to receive. During that time, I had also negotiated a severance package. Now, I asked my manager if that package was still on the table. He immediately made me an offer I could not refuse. I thought about my health, my family, and the endless difficulties at the organization, where "normal" was seemingly not in the vocabulary. It was not worth staying and fighting for a job in an organization that, for many reasons, I no longer believed in. I decided to take my severance and walk away.

Even though I had made my choice, I walked out of my office

feeling as though I had been thrown under a bus. I was no longer part of an organization to which I had devoted two years of my life—an organization in dire need of change, but one that did not care for what change looked and felt like. I had believed in its mission and did everything within my power to support it and help it become stronger and better, and yet, after two years and a steady series of promotions that had culminated in my appointment as director of human resources, I was unemployed.

Anyone who has experienced the loss of a job is familiar with the feelings of shock, confusion, self-doubt, and other emotions that swirled around in my mind during that time. I questioned myself relentlessly: Had I really done the right things? Was there any truth to the accusations, innuendoes, and half-truths that my superiors planned to use as reason for my termination? Did I, in some way, deserve to be out of a job? Was I being punished for violating the rules of some cosmic game that I didn't even know I was playing?

I ultimately chose not to stay and fight my separation, but I believed I had fought a good fight for two years, even though at times it seemed to be a losing battle.

One of my favorite movies of all time is *The Color Purple*. Some of the lines that I remember most are spoken by Sofia, the character portrayed by Oprah Winfrey. As she reflects on the many struggles she has faced, Sofia says, "All my life I had to fight..."[2]

That was exactly how I felt, especially in those early days after losing my job; it seemed to me that my life was one struggle right after another—most of them brought on by unfair opposition that came my way for doing what I believed to be right.

During those bewildering early days as I pondered my situation and reflected on the many skirmishes lost and won during my two years with my former employer, I found myself relying on my faith, the faith that has sustained me all my life. As I look back, I realize that having a foundation built on faith is probably what kept me sane and at least slightly centered as I waited for the ground to stop shifting beneath my feet. After all, faith is what gives us hope, and hope, as you'll see throughout this book, is the one thing no one can live without.

As my faith slowly began to reveal the story of who I really am deep down, I began to reach out for other stories, other narratives that could help me begin to make sense of this disruption that had been forced into my world by people and systems that somehow seemed bent on finding something bad, defective, and unacceptable about me.

As a professional woman who had spent many years in the corporate workplace, I'd heard all the cautionary tales: how women would never be able to genuinely take a seat at the table with men; how strong women who wouldn't display proper subservience to their male superiors—or peers—would eventually find themselves locked out of meaningful opportunities; how women—especially black women—almost always faced the choice of "playing nice" and being seen as unimaginative drones or standing up for their principles and being labeled uncooperative bitches. I had apparently landed in the latter category, and that was the reason I was now out of a job.

Was I the first woman in history who had found herself in this situation? As these new stories began to find their way to me, I learned that I most definitely was not alone in my predicament. In fact, I stood in a long line of women who "acted out": who refused to be defined by the stereotypes assembled by their patriarchal societies; who decided that their own dreams were better and more worthwhile than the dreams the rest of the world told them to have; who broke the rules and violated expectations in order to shout to a world that refused to listen, "I matter more than you think I do, and nothing you can do to me can change that!"

Listening to these stories of the brave, pioneering women who have gone before me has changed the way I see my experience. These stories have taken me on a journey of self-discovery and reevaluation ... a journey that has resulted in the writing of this book. And now, in these pages, I want to invite you to take the journey, too.

Women Who Misbehave

In her review of Laurel Thatcher Ulrich's wonderful book *Well-Behaved Women Seldom Make History*,[3] Kathryn Harrison of the *New York Times* wrote, "Much of what is characterized as female 'misbehavior' is a matter of voice—of a woman insisting she be heard: paid not only attention, but also the respect due a being as fully human and necessary as a man."[4] When I read these words, something resonated deep within me. And as I began a deeper examination into the stories of women who "misbehaved"—at least, according to the expectations of the surrounding society—I began to understand that what had happened to me was merely the tip of the iceberg of the type of mistreatment, misunderstanding, and outright hostility that women of all ethnicities have been exposed to since—well, since the beginning of time.

Even after the advances of the last few decades, women are still subjected to a type of scrutiny and cultural vetting that most men do not dream of and cannot understand. Reading the stories of women who have made a difference, who have overcome obstacles and shaken off societal shackles to pursue their dreams, has convinced me that despite the successes of the past, so much more remains to be done. And the doing—the striving, persisting, and succeeding—has to start with me. And with you.

So I suppose this book is, at least in part, the call to a struggle. But it is a struggle that is ultimately worthwhile, ultimately uplifting, and ultimately indispensible.

Beginning the Path: Hold onto Your Faith

In this struggle toward a redefinition of women's expectations and opportunities, the first step is to learn to rely on faith. This, after all, is what has empowered oppressed and misunderstood people throughout the ages. Faith gives us the ability to lift our eyes above the drab landscape of what is and imagine what could be. Faith inhabits the words of Sen. Edward (Ted) Kennedy, who in eulogizing his brother Robert, paraphrased a famous quote of George Bernard Shaw: "Some men see things as they are and say, 'Why?' I dream things that never were and say, 'Why not?'"[5] As long as you are able to hold onto your faith, you will always have a place to stand.

Choose Your Own Course

The next step you must take is determining to choose your own course. This only stands to reason; to walk the path of your own choosing, you must be certain, deep within yourself, that it is the path you have truly chosen to walk. Along the way, there will be many distractions, many voices that try to divert you, many fingers that point in accusation, trying to move you onto a different path. When you encounter such opposition, the only thing that will keep you moving in the direction of your dreams is the deep and certain conviction that you must follow your own choices, wherever they lead.

Rise above Limitations

Then, when your choice is fully formed within you, you must set yourself to rise above the limitations that others will inevitably seek to place on you. The source of these attempts to limit your achievements may surprise you, sometimes; they may come from those you considered friends—even family members. You may find, as I did, that by seeking to pursue your own dreams wherever they lead, you may cause others—often, those who lack the courage or perseverance to choose a similar path—to question or find fault with your decision or your objectives. Sometimes they will do this with expressions of concern for your "well-being," and other times they may resort to outright derision or accusation. Their motives may be centered in the unsettling sense of their own lack of direction or belief in themselves; if they can hold you back, it makes them feel better about remaining in the comfort of mediocrity.

Or, they may be, for various reasons, committed to the status quo and perceive your aspirations as a threat. For whatever reason they make the attempt, you must find the strength and inner vision to resist these limitations. Giving in to them will only weaken your resolve and slow your progress toward achieving your potential.

Persist against Opposition

At this point, it will probably come as no surprise to you to learn that opposition is inevitable. In fact, as you read the stories of the brave women who inspired my own beginning steps on this path, you will see that they were opposed at almost every stage. Some of the women you will read about in these pages paid a price in public mistrust and ridicule; some endured legal repression; a few even gave their lives as a result of their refusal to be diverted from their chosen paths. Fortunately, not many of us are likely to be called upon to make that ultimate sacrifice, but the common thread that unites all these women is that they persisted against unjust opposition, refusing to be cowed or intimidated into giving up on what they knew was right.

Speak Up for Justice

Perhaps as a result of the unjust obstacles placed in their paths, many of these women also became vocal opponents of injustice, wherever they saw it. You will see, in fact, that many of the rights we take for granted today were first championed by some of the women I have written about. If you choose this path, you, too, will likely become deeply sensitized by your experiences toward an instinctive dislike of unfairness and injustice. The more you are unwilling to be treated unfairly yourself, the less you will be able to sit idly by while others are treated unfairly—especially when those others have faces and names, as was the case with Ms. Vivian, a person whom you will meet a bit later in this book. Ms. Vivian was a person who had been written off by almost everyone, but as you'll see, by helping her, I actually received more than I gave.

Insist on Integrity

Another common thread I have noticed in the stories of the women who have inspired me is their insistence on integrity; to have the strength they needed to achieve their dreams, these women typically sink their roots deep in the spring of truth. At this point, I must admit that though all of the women in these pages have inspired me, I do not agree with all of them in every choice they have made. In fact, it may surprise some readers that I have drawn inspiration from figures as diverse as Sarah Palin and Hillary Rodham Clinton. And yet, even these two women, who are perhaps as opposite politically as anyone could be, have both inspired me with their determination to be true to themselves and to tell the truth about the world as they see it—regardless of the consequences. This willingness to tell the truth, no matter what, is what sets apart women of vision and determination. Part of the reason, which we will explore in more depth in a later chapter, is that truth, while indispensable for greatness, is also almost always inconvenient. While the Bible rightly says, "the truth shall set you free" (John 8:32), it is also a fact that often, telling the truth shall make you unpopular. However, for those who are determined to pursue their dreams and rise above externally imposed limitations, popularity is not the main thing; integrity is.

Keep Holding onto Your Faith

Finally, this passage cannot be attempted without a strong and deeply held faith. Some readers may think I am unwittingly repeating a point I made earlier, so let me say it this way: Faith is the beginning and the ending of the journey. In fact, faith inhabits every step along the way. I suggest that no individual who has accomplished something truly great has ever done so at the expense of his or her faith. Oh, I don't question that along the way, amid the heat of battle or the dry fatigue of discouragement, many, if not most, have probably wondered whether there was any ultimate purpose in the life they had chosen. In all honesty, I can tell you that in my dark times, I have certainly questioned my assumptions about God, about whether there was really any meaning to my struggles, about whether the universe might be a random, uncaring place after all. And in these dark times, I often seek inspiration and guidance from my faith.

Eventually, these moments of doubt pass, and belief reasserts itself, and hope is reborn, and we go on. In all of this, faith is the source; it enables us to keep going, keep hoping, keep believing, and keep trying.

An Invitation

And so, I again invite you to consider new possibilities with me in the pages of this book. I invite you to listen to the stories of these women who have been my guides, my examples, my teachers, and my inspiration. I invite you to allow their stories to enter your mind, to aid you in your own process of self-discovery and renewal.

I sometimes think that stories are the most indispensable things we have. Even if we had no computers, no machines, no cities … even if we had nothing left except our stories and the stories of the generations that have gone before us, I think that we would still have everything we need to become all that we can be. I think that stories not only tell us about other people—they tell us about ourselves as well. Stories change the way we think, the way we see. They show us things we never expected to notice. At least, that's the way it has been with me, as I began to encounter the stories of these incredible women who risked everything in order to become all they were capable of.

So if, like me, you have sometimes wondered if you really mattered or if there was something wrong with you because you couldn't find satisfaction or fulfillment in doing things the way everyone told you they'd always been done … you may find the beginnings of some answers in this book. As you learn of the difficulties, challenges, injustices, and triumphs experienced by the "misbehaving" women you will read about in this book, you may discover renewed determination to write your own story—the story with the best ending of all: the satisfaction of having done all that you were meant to do.

That's the dream I have for myself. I hope it's a dream you can share.

CHAPTER 1

Hold onto Your Faith

PERHAPS I SHOULD BEGIN THIS CHAPTER WITH A FEW WORDS OF EXPLANATION. I realize that not all readers will share my own adherence to the Christian faith, and I am not suggesting that they should. When I admonish you to hold onto your faith as you begin this journey toward your dreams, I am simply saying that without a deep core of belief, you will not be able to sustain your resolve against the tide of opposition that will inevitably come your way. As you progress down the path of self-determination, you will face resistance from society, from people in your life who are intimidated by or fearful of your decision, from misunderstanding superiors and peers ... and the list goes on. Without faith, the ability to believe in yourself and in the power that shapes your destiny, you will not be able to persist.

Why Faith Matters

Before I get into some specific instances of how faith has made a difference in my life and my journey towards self-discovery, it may be important to explain why I believe so adamantly that faith is the most essential attribute you must possess before setting your feet on the path toward your future. The simple fact is this: faith is not only your sustenance in hard times; it is also your compass.

Faith is the ability to perceive what cannot be seen—yet. The New Testament tells us, "Faith is the substance of things hoped for and the evidence of things not seen" (Hebrews 11:1). With faith, you are able to move forward even when the path is uncertain and the way is dark because your faith impels you with the belief that something better or more worthy lies ahead. Without faith, few of us would ever do anything of consequence because we would lack any reason to dare the uncertainty that always comes when we seek change from "the way things have always been." People who effect great change are and will always be people of faith; faith and great vision are inextricably linked in the human soul.

Another aspect of faith that makes it indispensable for people of vision is that faith, no matter its origin or guiding principle, is ultimately an intensely personal matter. If it weren't, it would have no power to move us to persevere and accomplish great things.

As evidence and explanation of these observations about faith, I want to relate a bit about how my faith sustained me during the difficult days immediately following my separation from my employer. My process and the course of my journey will no doubt look different than yours, and the terms I use to describe it are likely not the same that you would use. However, I hope that by learning a bit about my experiences, you can come to understand on your own terms how essential it is to have a faith that can sustain you when life seems to have taken everything else away.

My Own "Dark Night of the Soul"

As I mentioned in the introduction to this book, my own faith in God was what sustained me in the days and weeks immediately following the loss of my job. However, the fact that I was sustained does not mean that I was comfortable; it does not mean that I did not go through times of deep soul-searching. After all, what I experienced on that cold, crisp November day was painful, and while I am no stranger to pain or suffering, this experience jolted me to the core. In the process of recovery, I had to discover who I was and redefine my life. Along the way, I also experienced what is known to many as the "dark night of the soul." As I was going through this difficult time, I constantly questioned and even blamed God for the pain I was experiencing. To be honest, I was angry with God and I had no problems expressing my feelings of anger towards him. I wanted answers for the painful circumstances I was experiencing—yet God was silent, as far as I could tell.

I was at a crossroads, in more ways than one! First of all, I had to decide whether or not I wanted to continue in the same line of work or find something to do that would be more meaningful and satisfying. I was bored and restless. I had received a year's worth of severance, but I was accustomed to going to work each day, as I had done since I was seventeen. Sitting idle was not part of my plan! I sent out dozens of résumés—after a while I lost count of the number—but got just as many rejections. Each rejection made me more anxious; I worried about what would happen if I could not pay the mortgage on my home or the loan on my vehicle. I even looked for temporary assignments, and though some seemed promising, none of them worked out. I had worked really hard for everything that I had accomplished, and had always believed that God had allowed me to have the things I did, but now it seemed that doors were closing, one after the other.

During these times, I had no peace and no joy. I began journaling as a way to express my pain and confusion, and while that helped a great deal, many nights I could not sleep. Where are you, God? I asked, over and over. My faith assured me of God's promises—he would deliver me and comfort me in my darkest hour, yet it seemed he was silent. It felt as though God had me in a wrestler's hold with my face in the mat; no matter how hard I tried, I could not break free to see the light of day.

Often I felt like giving up, but something within me just could not let go of my faith. I could not let go of what I had been taught or the times when I had been blessed beyond measure. Still, I longed for the good times I enjoyed with God and yearned to have a peaceful relationship with him. But now ... it seemed as if heaven was closed off and no sound was coming from above.

Much of the above may sound pretty hopeless for a Chapter that's supposed to be about holding onto your faith. However, one thing I've learned is that any faith that's tough enough to sustain you has to be able to stand up to some times of doubt and deep self-questioning. At some point, the turn back towards hope will come, and that's how it was with me.

As I reflected on the chain of events that got me to this low point in my life, I continued to believe that I had done the right thing; however, during my pain and suffering, what I experienced was brokenness. I came to understand that my struggle was not primarily about me or what I had experienced, but was rather about the fact that I was headed into unfamiliar territory, being forced out of my comfort zone. I was also being purged of all those things that I had become dependent on so that God, who longed for a deeper relationship with me, could lead me to be dependent on him. In the time before losing my job, as I began to climb the corporate ladder, I became dependent on myself and my abilities. I came to believe that God was seeking to remind me of the true source of my strength and my abilities.

One thing I learned during this difficult process was that God does not make mistakes. The process of purging and pruning is painful; however, I learned to trust God more completely, and as a result, my faith became stronger. Still, this was one of the darkest passages that I ever experienced in my life. I wept until I thought I was unable to weep any more; I continued to feel anger towards God. But in the end, I remembered the words of the song that was in my mind on the morning of November 11, 2009: "No matter what may come my way, my life is in your hands."[1] I recalled and relied upon the stories of my faith: of Joseph, who endured betrayal by his own family and false accusations that led to imprisonment, yet God promoted him to the second highest position in the land; of Job, who endured the loss of everything and everyone he held dear, but held fast to his belief—and God restored to him everything that he lost.

And so, though my experience caused me to question everything I knew about God, and though many times I felt like throwing in the towel, God never gave up on me. For me, that understanding was key to surviving the feelings of shame, loss, anger, and resentment, and moving on to a place of greater understanding.

I Am Not Alone

While it is certainly true that being the target of sexism and other types of "isms" is painful on a personal level, my experiences forced me to look at the bigger picture—to see my situation not only in light of its effects on my life, but on the wider implications for other people. So, in addition to learning to have greater reliance on my faith, I also found comfort in the stories of other women who faced sexism, racism, ageism, and other types of obstacles intended to discourage them and make them fail. As you will see in the remaining chapters of this book, they persevered in spite of persecution. They, too, relied on their faith—however that faith was expressed in each woman's life. For many of them, faith in God was key to survival and persistence. For others, faith took the form of holding onto a belief in the value of the ideas or causes they were fighting for. In other words, not all of the women who have fought back against a repressive society or an unfair system have found their strength, as I did, in a personal relationship with the God of the Judeo-Christian tradition.

Indeed, many people today—including many women—mistrust the Judeo-Christian faith tradition, citing it as one of the greatest historical allies of bigotry and oppression, including the oppression of women. These observations are not without basis in fact. Throughout history, the Bible has been used to justify patriarchal cultural patterns that seek to keep women "in their place." Many churches still do not permit women to exercise the same types of leadership roles and oversight that are available to men. There are many churches where women are not allowed to preach or to teach men. Many women also feel that the beliefs and attitudes towards women's roles and responsibilities in the church have been transferred to women in corporate America, where often the roles considered appropriate for women are not those of leaders but rather those of submissive followers.

Many cultures view women as inferior to men, and their roles are limited to being wives and mothers. In some instances, men have used scriptures to develop laws, charters, or policies for their organizations that perpetuate subservience as the "proper" attitude for a woman.

However, scripture is read and interpreted by humans—and often misinterpreted. Just because a particular interpretation is traditional does not guarantee that it is also accurate. As I read the Bible, for instance, I find much evidence that oppression of women is a doctrine that originated in the minds of men, not the mind of God. I suppose that the holy writings of all the world's major religions are often used incorrectly by humans in an effort to advance themselves or their own viewpoints. I am most familiar with the Bible, of course, and I find it particularly troubling that its teachings of love and mutual respect are often drowned out by those who wish to justify unfair treatment for one group or another.

Whether you are a believer in the Judeo-Christian tradition or not, however, many of the same principles apply when we consider the ways that religion has been misused and misunderstood in ways that result in the repression of women. Perhaps a few examples from the Bible can illustrate this point.

What the Bible Says—and Doesn't Say—about Women

In the book of Genesis, for example, Eve, the first woman created, received the responsibility of co-managing all of creation with her husband. Eve was also made in God's image and had the characteristics of God. She had an important role together with her husband, which was the continuation of creation. Some traditionalists point to God's words to her following the temptation and Fall—"he will rule over you"—as justification for the domination of women by men. However, other scholars point out that these words came *after* the Fall. Thus, they do not represent God's intentions in the perfect world that he envisioned. In the perfect plan of God, they reason, Adam and Eve were co-equals before God; they shared the role of creation. Only when that perfection was disrupted did male/female hierarchy result. I believe that we should recapture in our own time that Paradise vision of what God originally intended between men and women: equality, not repression.

Throughout the Old Testament, God uses women, some virtuous and some not so virtuous, to advance his plans for humankind. Queens, matriarchs, servant girls, and even prostitutes figure prominently in the unfolding of God's will in the pages of scripture. We'll meet one or two of these women a little later on in this chapter.

In fact, much of the imagery used for God in the Bible is female imagery. In Psalm 131, the writer describes the comfort of the human soul in God's presence in these terms: "I have stilled and quieted my soul; like a weaned child with its mother ...." In Isaiah 14, God, speaking through the prophet, says, "Can a mother forget the baby at her breast and have no compassion on the child she has borne? Though she may forget, I will not forget you!" And in the New Testament, Jesus, speaking for God, looks at the city of Jerusalem and describes the way he longs to care for his people. Matthew 23:37 records his words this way: "... how often I have longed to gather your children together, as a hen gathers her chicks under her wings, but you were not willing." Clearly, these feminine images for God don't fall in line with the stern, patriarchal images of God that males have used through the centuries to keep women "in line."

The stories of Jesus also reveal many surprising truths about the way his interactions with women lifted them up to their proper place rather than keeping them under the heels of their brothers, husbands, and fathers. Women played an important role in Jesus' ministry and, in fact, were part of his inner circle. Wealthy women provided some portion—perhaps a substantial portion—of the monetary support for his itinerant ministry. There are no instances or examples found in the New Testament where Jesus marginalized women or treated them unfairly or with disrespect. Most of Jesus' interactions with women were to teach, uplift, heal, deliver, and liberate them. In several of the gospels, we see Jesus speaking to women publicly (the Samaritan woman at the well, for example) or having interactions with women that the surrounding society—including some of his male followers—viewed as inappropriate (such as Mary Magdalene).

In many instances, Jesus went against what was customary or even lawful in his culture: he healed on the Sabbath; he touched lepers and the dead; and he taught and spoke to women. On one famous occasion, he publicly opposed the teachers of religious law and Pharisees who brought before him a woman caught in the act of adultery. Instead of condemning her, as would have been easy and popular, he said, "Let the one among you who is without sin cast the first stone" (John 8:7). And they all walked away, very quietly.

As I read that story, I've always wondered: where was the man who was having sex with the woman? Wasn't he just as guilty as she was? And yet, in the Jewish culture of first-century Palestine, the woman's guilt seemed to be all that mattered to her accusers. But the woman, herself, was what mattered most to Jesus, it seems.

It's also important to note that it was a group of women who stood at the foot of the cross, watching Jesus die and hearing his last words.

During the crucifixion, there were women who followed Jesus from Galilee after most of the men fled. Women were the first ones at the tomb after his resurrection and he appeared first to women after his resurrection: Matthew 28:9–10 describes how Mary Magdalene and "the other Mary" were the first followers of Jesus to meet him after his resurrection. It is clear that women played a full and vibrant role in the ministry of Jesus, both as examples within his teaching and as recipients of it. While this may seem absolutely right and proper in our twenty-first–century context, we must remember how radical this was in first-century Palestine. For example, in this society the word of women had less value than that of men. Women's testimony was not admissible in the rabbinical courts, for example. It is therefore enormously important that the significant events of Jesus' death and resurrection were first witnessed primarily by women.

Paul, one of the most important figures in the earliest days of the Church, also had some attitudes toward women that might be considered unusual for his day. For example, he wrote in a letter to the churches in Galatia (modern Turkey), "There is neither Jew nor Greek, slave nor free, male nor female, for you are all one in Christ Jesus" (Galatians 3:28). A truly radical teaching for a society bound by gender, ethnicity, and class (wait a minute ... that sounds like our society today!). Paul also had women in his inner circle, notably Priscilla, the wife of Paul's fellow tentmaker, Aquila. Priscilla is a dominant figure in Paul's ministry, on one occasion assisting her husband in teaching the young evangelist Apollos some doctrinal matters that he apparently did not know (Acts 18:24).

The New Testament ascribes numerous roles to women in the early Church: teachers of theology, deacons, church leaders, and prophets. There is even a disputed reference to a female apostle called Junia.

While it is true to say that there are two particular passages in Paul's writings that seem to go against all of this by commanding some women to be silent and forbidding others from teaching, these must be read and interpreted in their specific context. Paul also gives guidelines for women to use when they publicly prophesy and also affirms women who teach, like Priscilla.

In summary, I find it frustrating that many of the scriptures that are taken out of context are usually the ones used to marginalize or oppress someone's race, status, or gender, while ignoring one of the greatest and clearest commandments: to love your neighbor as yourself. That is an ideal that anyone can espouse, no matter which religion he or she practices—even if none.

An Unlikely Role Model

Earlier I mentioned the stories of women throughout history who have inspired me and enabled me to better understand my place in the world and my yearning to make the world a better place for everyone, regardless of race or gender. It may surprise you to find out that one of my greatest heroes in this regard is a woman found in the Bible ... a prostitute named Rahab.

Jesus once said, "What does it profit a person to gain the whole world but lose his or her soul?" (Matthew 16:26). When we meet her, Rahab was in danger of losing her soul in her efforts to gain the world. Like many of us, Rahab had a job that was degrading and deadening to her spirit. We may not have sold our bodies; however, many of us have sold our souls, sold out others, or sold out to organizations to obtain profit or advancement.

Have you been put in a position where you had to choose between right and wrong and you chose to do what was wrong because it was the popular choice? What do you do when you realize that your company or organization is headed down the wrong path, and despite your best efforts to help save the organization, you realize you are fighting a losing battle—do you stay and go down with the Titanic? What if you are the messenger of ill or even good tidings, but your idea or opinion is not valued because of your age, gender, race, or sexual orientation? Do you keep trying to be heard and hope you will get your boss's attention? Do you go to your boss's boss? What if your boss is the owner of the company or head of the organization? If you decide to leave an organization because you no longer believe in their vision or they exhibit behaviors that are not in line with your personal values, does it mean that you are a traitor? Believe it or not, we can learn some answers to each of these questions by considering the career of Rahab, the Madam of Jericho.

The Old Testament book of Joshua introduces us to Rahab, one of the most famous, provocative, and amazing women in the ancient world. She was immoral, yet as a result of her great faith and her actions she would go on to earn a place in the Bible's "Hall of Fame." In Hebrews 11, the Bible says, "By faith the prostitute Rahab, because she welcomed the spies, was not killed with those who were disobedient." Rahab is even listed in the lineage of Christ as found in Matthew 1:5.

The story of Rahab takes place during the time in which the Israelites were beginning their conquest of the Promised Land of Canaan. Jericho was a wealthy city in the Jordan Valley, and word was getting around that the wandering marauders, led by Joshua and Co., were in the neighborhood.

In fact, Israelite spies were sent to probe Jericho's weaknesses in preparation for the attack. Their presence was suspected, however, and the authorities put out an all-points bulletin for the good folk of Jericho to be on the lookout for these agents of the advancing enemy. The spies, needing a place to hide, did what fugitives have done for millennia; they headed for the seedy side of town, where people don't ask so many questions. Eventually, they found themselves at Rahab's place. After all, there are few establishments anywhere that offer more anonymity than a whorehouse.

The Bible provides very little information on Rahab's life prior to her encounter with the spies. Was she a prostitute because of choice or was she forced into it by circumstance? Why did she choose this profession? We don't really know. I often wonder what Rahab's childhood was like, who her role models were while she was growing up and the reasons behind the choices she made. Was she molested as a child? Was she promiscuous? Maybe she had a wonderful childhood, but possessed a rebellious nature. Maybe she was not satisfied with the career choices available to women at that time. Maybe she felt she could earn more money selling her body than she would earn harvesting flax. Did she feel obligated to take care of her family as a result of poverty? What did her daddy think of his little girl being a prostitute? What about the women whose husbands utilized her services? Did they blame their husbands, or did they blame Rahab? Did she keep a little black book with her clients' information? Nevertheless, Rahab's current situation and profession was not the end of her story. Her degrading profession, one in which she sold her body and was disrespected by her clients and society, ended up being used in God's purpose and plan for her life.

Not all business is good business—or is it? When the spies contacted Rahab, she probably thought to herself, "Oh, great, more clients." Nevertheless, the Bible says that she not only allowed them into her premises, she also hid them from the authorities:

> But the woman had taken the two men and hidden them; and she said, "True, men came to me, but I did not know where they came from; and when the gate was to be closed, at dark, the men went out; where the men went I do not know. (Joshua 2:4)

So, not only was Rahab a prostitute but she was a liar as well. It is possible that lying was an occupational necessity for Rahab; she was probably accustomed to keeping men's secrets from their wives and families. Lying was part of her business. Though clever, it was also risky for her to send the soldiers on a wild goose chase. By lying, Rahab clearly put her life at risk. In many of our professions, we sometimes lie to protect the bottom line of the organization; however, the last decade has taught us that lying is not an option when it is used to deceive the public or for fraudulent gain. Enron and WorldCom are notorious examples of how lying and deceit can destroy lives and organizations. And yet many people attempt to deceive for one reason or another. Before we pass judgment, however, we need to put ourselves in another person's shoes. What would drive us to put our lives and careers at risk by lying—or by telling the truth? In this instance, Rahab lied.

What would make Rahab risk her own life to protect the lives of strangers that she did not know? The Bible gives no indication that the men paid for or utilized Rahab's services, so she was apparently not protecting them as clients. The Bible gives us an insight into her motivation, however:

> Before they lay down, she came up to them on the roof, and said to the men, "I know that the Lord has given you the land, and that the fear of you has fallen upon us, and that all the inhabitants of the land melt away before you. For we have heard how the Lord dried up the water of the Red Sea before you when you came out of Egypt, and what you did to the two kings of the Amorites that were beyond the Jordan, to Sihon and Og, whom you utterly destroyed. And as soon as we heard it, our hearts melted, and there was no courage left in any man, because of you; for the Lord your God is he who is God in heaven above and on earth beneath." (Joshua 2:8–11)

The corporate world understands the importance of business acumen. Rahab was an intelligent woman, likely familiar with politics and the issues affecting the society in which she lived. After all, she rubbed shoulders—and more than shoulders—with a clientele that in all likelihood contained some of the "Who's Who" of Jericho's society. Rahab clearly had a sense of which direction the winds of change were blowing, and as the story reveals, she had already made up her mind about which camp she preferred to be in when push came to shove. Notice her next words to the Israelite spies:

> Now then, swear to me by the Lord that as I have dealt kindly with you, you also will deal kindly with my father's house, and give me a sure sign, and save

> alive my father and mother, my brothers and sisters, and all who belong to them, and deliver our lives from death. (Joshua 2:12, 13)

Quid pro quo! Rahab was, after all, an entrepreneur with connections, business acumen, and negotiating skills. She demonstrated no hesitation as she put these talents into practice by negotiating for her life and the life of her family.

Did it work?

> And the men said to her, "Our life for yours! If you do not tell this business of ours, then we will deal kindly and faithfully with you when the Lord gives us the land." Then she let them down by a rope through the window, for her house was built into the city wall, so that she dwelt in the wall. And she said to them, "Go into the hills, lest the pursuers meet you; and hide yourselves there three days, until the pursuers have returned; then afterward you may go your way."
>
> The men said to her, "We will be blameless of this oath of yours which you have made us swear, unless, when we come into the land, you bind this line of scarlet cord in the window through which you let us down, and unless you bring your father, your mother, your brothers, and all your father's household to your own home. Then she said, "According to your words, so be it." And she sent them away, and they departed. And she bound the scarlet cord in the window. (Joshua 2:14–21)

I can't help wondering what Rahab was feeling, given the knowledge she was carrying. She had a huge burden to bear; getting her entire family to her house without revealing the reason, for example, was probably no easy task. What if the Israelite spies did not keep their promise to her? Events in Rahab's house probably became chaotic, given the preparations she was making to have herself and her family rescued. No doubt, this was matched by the chaos in the city, since Jericho was preparing for imminent war. How did all this fear and uncertainty affect Rahab's business? And what feelings did she have about this city that had been her home for all the years before? Clearly, Rahab believed she was on the losing team and was putting her exit strategy into play. What emotions did this trigger within her? Did she feel like a traitor, or did she congratulate herself on being shrewd enough to pull off this great switch of allegiance without getting caught?

Many Bible scholars believe that the scarlet cord represented more than just a rope for climbing up or down the wall; the scarlet cord may also have been a symbol of Rahab's profession, similar to the red light sometimes used today to identify brothels. But in this case, the red cord also symbolized a promise between Rahab and the spies, a promise of deliverance from the impending destruction of the city and Rahab's life of prostitution. After Jericho was destroyed, the Bible declares, "Joshua spared Rahab the harlot, her father's household, and all that she had—and she lives among the Israelites to this day" (Joshua 6:25).

The story of Rahab amazes and inspires me. Even though its main character is a woman of ill repute, it contains elements of hope, promise, deliverance, family loyalty, and love. I also find it fascinating that Rahab's name is mentioned in several different books of the Bible (Joshua, Matthew, Hebrews, and James) partly because of her profession but mainly for her faith and her incredible insight and willingness to assist the Israelite spies because she knew the Lord had given her city to the Israelites.

Before you make any type of life-changing decision, consider the cost! Rahab put her life and the life of her family at risk. In many ways, she turned her back on the very people who had supported her business through the years. However, she wanted a better life and knew that the degrading profession in which she had spent so many years did not define her. Her faith allowed her to see above the horizon of her own experience and move decisively when a better opportunity presented itself. Rahab, as it turns out, was a woman of vision who charted a course for herself that was very different than anything most of the people around her would have ever expected her to choose. Instead of sitting back and waiting for something to happen, Rahab seized the day and made something happen.

In the same way, many women have the desire to mark out their own paths rather than meekly treading the course society, tradition, or culture has laid out for them. Like Rahab, they sense that there are greater and better opportunities available for the taking by those who have the faith to see them and the courage to step forward and claim them. In fact, we can find examples of women who have done just that—much more recently than Rahab! Let's turn now to the stories of some of the women who took this next step along the path to their destinies—women who made the decision to chart their own courses.

CHAPTER 2

Choose Your Own Course

As I reflect on the difficulties I faced in the weeks and months prior to my separation from my former employer, I recall many occasions when I had to choose between going along with practices and policies that I knew to be inefficient, unproductive, or completely wrong and standing up for what I believed to be the right way to do things. In many cases, these decisions placed me at odds with my superiors. I'm sure there were times when backing down—or at least modifying my expectations temporarily—would have made my life easier. But in almost every case, I chose to continue pressing for accuracy, fairness, best practices, and efficiency, all the while knowing I was likely placing myself at the bottom of the popularity polls—at least, as far as my bosses were concerned.

While I don't regard myself as any sort of hero for doing what I believed was both proper and in the best interests of my organization, I do recognize that in much of corporate America, "go along/get along" is the tacitly accepted rule of the road, especially for women. We are expected to comply, be good soldiers, take one for the team, and salute the colors on the way out the door. To think for ourselves, or, heaven forbid, to refuse to bow to the wishes of the organization, however misguided they are, almost always makes us suspect in the eyes of the powers that be. In other words, to insist on our own rights of independent thought and action is to do the unexpected, even the unthinkable.

As I have encountered the stories of women who "misbehave," I have discovered that most if not all of them did what was considered unthinkable—at least for a woman—during their lives. They dared to defy cultural expectations in order to chart their own courses in history. And in so doing, they have changed our world.

As you read the stories of a few of these women, I invite you to imagine your own course. What might you accomplish—in your home, your workplace, your community—if there was no one who could stop you or stand in your way? As you consider those possibilities, I challenge you to take the next step: dare to define your own possibilities, rather than continue to allow others to define them for you. As you meet some of the women who have inspired me as they dared to reject stereotyping and societal definition, allow their courage to find its way into your heart and (re)kindle your dreams.

Golda Meir: Mother Figure for a Nation at War

> *"Trust yourself. Create the kind of self that you will be happy to live with all your life. Make the most of yourself by fanning the tiny, inner sparks of possibility into flames of achievement."*

These words, spoken by Golda Meir, capture the essence of a life spent in pursuit of destiny. It is true that Golda Meir has been criticized as a "queen bee": a woman who climbed to the top and then pulled the ladder up after her. Historians have found fault with her refusal to use her position of authority to advocate for the rights of women in general. And yet, her example remains as undeniable proof that women are every bit as capable, resourceful, and tough, when called upon to be so, as their male counterparts.

Golda Meir was the first woman prime minister to lead Israel and the third woman prime minister in history. Born in the Ukraine in 1898, Meir moved with her family to the United States to escape the religious persecution being carried out against Jews in the region. The immigrant family resided in a poor Jewish community near Milwaukee. As a teenager, she had many struggles between remaining true to herself and staying on the path her parents—especially her father—wanted her to follow. While Golda Mabovitch—as she was then known—wanted to go to high school and had dreams of becoming a teacher, her parents wanted her to follow a more traditional role that involved finding a husband and becoming a mother. "It doesn't pay to be too clever," her father reportedly warned her, "men don't like smart girls."[1]

Reflecting on my own childhood, I was always told by my parents that I could achieve anything I wanted in life—the sky is the limit; however, there are many of us who can relate to Golda's struggles. We have goals and dreams that are not always shared by our loved ones or well-meaning individuals whom we consider role models. For various reasons, these well-meaning individuals often want us to follow the defined paths they mapped out for our lives. Some of us have parents who want to live out their dreams through us because they either missed or never received an opportunity to live their own dreams. I had a teacher in high school who felt that I was getting too big for my britches and told me that I would not amount to anything. I remembered being hurt and disappointed at hearing these words from a teacher; however, I did not let it distract me from what my parents taught me. Words can often pierce like a sword, and if used in a destructive manner they can hurt to the core and can tear down one's self-esteem.

Golda's parents probably had a traditional view of what a woman's role should be—wife and mother. Maybe her mother was aware of the struggles many women faced for equality and wanted to spare her the pain and disappointments she would encounter along the way. Perhaps there were not many women role models who lived out their dreams and aspirations during that time.

Golda's parents probably never imagined that their little girl would become prime minister of Israel. Against her parents' wishes, however, Golda decided to pursue her dreams and attended high school in Milwaukee in the hopes of becoming a teacher. As a result, she faced ongoing conflict with her parents over her dreams of following a non-traditional path and finally ran away from home to live with her sister and brother-in-law in Denver.

Living with her sister and brother-in-law, Meir was exposed to different views, some of which were radical and would later create the framework for her future political aspirations. In additional to being exposed to a different worldview, she also acquired an appreciation of literature and history as a result of her relationship with Morris Myerson, who shared many of Golda's passions. They also shared a commitment to Zionism and eventually married in December 1917. After graduating from high school, Golda enrolled in a teacher's preparatory program in Milwaukee to prepare for teaching; however, her political yearnings were becoming more apparent and in 1921 the couple made *aliyah* to Palestine in order to join a kibbutz. In Palestine, Meir worked for the labor movement and held several positions.

Meir's political aspirations were driven by her passion for politics and a love for her people. She never thought that her gender was a handicap that would limit her from achieving her goals. She was determined to be successful at every position she held. I always admire women who are aware of the limitations placed on them by society but who persist in spite of the odds. They believe they are as good as anyone and do not view their gender as a limiting force but rather a force to be reckoned with. Golda was that reckoning force. Her work within the labor movement did not go unnoticed—it led her to achieve various political positions including diplomatic missions in the United States and other countries.

Meir's various roles and positions gave her a unique perspective on how she viewed the world and her place in it. She did not always support what was popular; she worked for or opposed causes that could have easily ended her career or even put her life at risk. She led efforts to oppose the British White Paper of 1939, which sought to limit Jewish emigration to Palestine. During World War II, she held several key positions in the World Zionist Organization and in the Jewish Agency, the highest Jewish authority in British-administered Palestine. She also placed herself at great risk by organizing illegal Jewish immigration to Palestine when Jews were being persecuted in Europe by Fascist and Nazi regimes. This illegal activity led the British to arrest those involved in the smuggling of refugees to Palestine. As a result, the male leadership of the Jewish Agency was arrested and Meir assumed the role as the interim head and was responsible for communicating with the British.

In spite of all the opposition and risks involved, Meir never gave up. She understood the risks; however, she played an instrumental role in helping her beloved Israel become a state and was among the signers of its Declaration of Independence.

There are many who believe that women are too emotional to be leaders and do not respond well under pressure; however, I believe great leaders are leaders because of their ability to inspire, because of their passion, their decision-making skills, their compassion, their insight, and their integrity. Leadership is not and should not be based on one's gender. Golda was a leader.

After Israel became a state in 1948, Meir was later elected to the Parliament (*Knesset*), and held the positions of Minister of Labor and Minister of Foreign Affairs—the only woman in the labor ministry. The "Myerson Plan" was named after her, as she was responsible for the construction of more than thirty thousand one-room housing units. She also spearheaded the construction of hundreds of thousands of low-income apartments for the mass Jewish immigration of families to Israel. Her leadership and dedication to causes in which she had a deep passion led then–Prime Minister David Ben-Gurion to refer to Meir as "the best man in the cabinet."[2]

I find it ironic when women are likened to men because their performance is exemplary or when they achieve greatness. There is a very popular saying—"Act like a lady think like a man"—that many women have latched onto, not realizing that it is somewhat degrading. Why do I have to think like a man in order to be great or strategic? Isn't the advantage of diversity its ability to offer unique perspectives from another person's perspective, background, culture, race, gender, and so forth? Yet many women consider it a badge of honor to be likened to a man or to possess what are considered male characteristics.

Many young girls have a passion for sports but are often prevented from playing because of their gender; they are told they should play in an all-women's league. In some sports an all-women's league does not exist; however, the girls do not consider their gender as limiting—they just want to play the game. Usually their safety is a concern, but their gender is the reason for the exclusion.

It is not clear whether or not then–Prime Minister David Ben-Gurion's comment was a term of endearment based on Golda's accomplishments, but it is clear he saw her as "one of the guys" instead of viewing her as a great leader who just happened to be a woman. Incidentally, Ben-Gurion's desire to have all Israelis bear Hebrew names resulted in Golda reluctantly changing her name from Meyerson to Meir.[3]

During the decades of British administration of Palestine, many clashes had occurred between Arab Palestinians and Jews as a result of disputes over land and political control. Israel suffered guerilla attacks on Jewish settlements that escalated the threat of war with the Arab nations. Meir worked diligently to raise funds to equip Israel's army. She solicited money from the various Jewish communities in the United States and raised millions to equip the military to defend Israel against the Arabs.

In 1948, she risked her life by disguising herself as a Muslim woman (not a man) and crossing into Jordan to meet with King Abdullah to persuade him against going to war with Israel. Despite his respect and admiration for Meir, she was not able to convince him to stay out of the war. He reportedly asked her not to be in a hurry to proclaim the State of Israel, and she is said to have replied, "We've been waiting for 2,000 years. Is that hurrying?"[4]

Meir's appointment as Israeli ambassador to the Soviet Union was a significant responsibility because her earliest memories included seeing her father shutter the family's business in Ukraine because of fear of an imminent pogrom and fleeing to the United States. Prime Minister Ben-Gurion named her to the second highest position in the government in 1956: foreign minister—the only woman in the world to hold such a position during that time.

Meir was admired for her many accomplishments as well as her diplomacy and humility. She never let her accomplishments go to her head. She had the opportunity to demand certain luxuries as a result of her position; however, she reportedly refused to fly first-class and was also known to hand-wash her own underwear and shine her own shoes.

After accomplishing many firsts and serving her country honorably, she retired from the government at age sixty-eight. During this time and unknown to many, Meir had been diagnosed with lymphoma. This was a different battle and a different kind of enemy; however, she was not about to go out without a fight. Her greatest fight, however, was still ahead.

You can take the lady out of politics but you can't take the politics out of the lady. Shortly after her retirement, she was strongly encouraged to assume several key roles within her political party, Mapai, and would go on to assume the position of secretary general of Mapai. She later became secretary of the Unified Labor Party.

After the death of Prime Minister Levi Eshkol in 1969 a power struggle ensued within the party, and in order to maintain stability and to keep the party from falling apart, Meir was tapped to become Israel's Prime Minister. In becoming Prime Minister, Meir accomplished a role that many coveted, and shattered the glass ceiling. This appointment came during a difficult time in Israel's history involving the ongoing conflict with Israel's Arab neighbors and an impending war. Egypt and Syria attacked Israel on October 6, 1973, the start of what is known as the Yom Kippur War (it began on Yom Kippur, the Day of Atonement, the holiest day of prayer and fasting in the Jewish calendar). Egyptian and Syrian military forces launched a surprise attack, knowing that the religious celebrations associated with Yom Kippur meant that Israel's borders were less heavily guarded.

The combat was fierce, but Israel, with financial, intelligence, and other assistance from the United States, managed to mount an offensive and to defeat their enemies.

Even though Israel won the war, Meir faced a new battle for not doing more to protect the borders. Meir would later regret not following her instincts to call up the reserves earlier and for heavily relying on the advice she received from military intelligence, which advised against mobilization.

This is a learning opportunity for many of us who are faced with decisions and subsequently bow to pressure. The position of leader requires us to work strategically and collaboratively with others; however, the ultimate decision is with the person in charge. Golda went against her better judgment and had to face the consequences. The backlash and outcry from the citizens was tremendous. She lost support and approval from many of her earlier supporters as they blamed her for the death of their loved ones. No longer "unified," the Unified Labor Party knew there was little they could to do to recover from the public outcry. As a great leader, Golda understood the war happened on her watch and took full responsibility for the humiliation and pain that resulted. She did not blame military intelligence for the bad advice she received, and in 1974 she resigned from office. Despite the public outcry, however, Golda Meir would go on to become one of the most beloved figures in Israel's history.

Although she was the first woman to accomplish many firsts in history, she was often criticized by women because she did not identify herself as a feminist. Many women felt Meir had the power and position to help other women get ahead; however, she failed to do so. They felt that Meir should have understood better than most the pressure to conform to traditional roles as well as the struggles she faced when her parents wanted her to assume traditional roles despite her own dreams and desires to forge her own path and chart her own course. These struggles should have led her to do more to help other women who shared similar urges to forge their own paths.

As with many of the women Betty Friedan wrote about in *The Feminine Mystique,* Meir reportedly felt isolated in the years following the birth of her children as she also struggled with her duty to her family and her desire to follow her own course, which in Meir's case involved her duty to serve her nation. Meir reportedly wrote about the guilt faced by some modern women because of their lack of satisfaction with traditional gender roles and their impulse toward the pursuit of self-fulfillment—seen by some as abandonment of their families; however, she refused to advocate for or support women's rights. Many believed that her refusal to support women's rights was due to her desire to be "one of the boys." She saw herself as a leader who happened to be a woman, not a female leader, according to some.

Knesset member Colette Avital, who began her career under Meir's leadership, says of Meir, "To survive Israeli politics she had to become tough, she had no choice; she must have gone through hell to get where she did." During the height of the second wave of feminism in the United States, Meir was voted "Most Admired Woman in America" and was hailed as a "poster child" for feminism.[5]

By all accounts, Meir understood the important role women played in the founding of the State of Israel. She was the perfect example and role model for women around the world, given the struggles she faced being a woman in a "man's world." As prime minister, she was in the perfect position to advocate for many of the issues and policies women were fighting for, such as childcare and gender equality. As a working mother, she understood the systems women were up against as well as the guilt many women felt when not conforming to traditional roles. Like Meir, there are many women who have achieved important roles, status, and positions; however, they refuse to help or mentor other women who are faced with obstacles similar to those they faced along the way. Many of these women refuse to identify themselves primarily as women and choose instead to be "one of the boys" because they believe acting like a man is the reason for their accomplishments.

According to various reports, when Ben-Gurion described Meir as "the best man" in his cabinet, Meir evidenced amusement that he thought "this was the greatest possible compliment that could be paid to a woman. I very much doubt that any man would have been flattered if I had said about him that he was the best woman in the government!"[6] In other words, she noticed the disparity in attitudes but seemed to miss the larger point.

Golda Meir died on December 8, 1978, at age eighty. She will always be known as one of the most accomplished women in the world. What would have happened to Meir's historical accomplishments if she had chosen the path defined for her by her parents or if she accepted the roles society defined for her? What if she had believed her father when he said, "It doesn't pay to be too clever," or, "men don't like smart girls"?[7]

Shannon Faulkner: Shattering Gender Barriers

> *"I was good enough for them. They looked at my academic record and said I was an ideal candidate."*

Shannon Faulkner was, indeed, good enough to be accepted for enrollment in 1993 at the Citadel, a previously all-male military academy located in South Carolina. Steeped in tradition, the Citadel was founded in the 1820s and prides itself on its quality education, toughness, and discipline. The Citadel also prides itself on its cadets being the first to fire shots at a Union ship in the Civil War. Among its alumni are twelve U.S. congressmen, six governors, three U.S. senators, an astronaut, and a number of three-and four-star generals. With the enrollment of Shannon Faulkner, its first female cadet, this institution steeped in tradition was about to face a battle of another type—an internal struggle against gender prejudice and resistance to change that would shake it to its foundations—and make of Shannon Faulkner at various times a scapegoat, an object of hatred, a hero, a survivor, and a victim.

The Citadel, a state-funded institution, excluded women from its corps of cadets for about 151 years. However, in 1993, Shannon Faulkner was accepted for admission, based on her qualifications as presented on her admission application. She reportedly omitted her gender, and her guidance counselors were instructed to omit any reference to gender on her transcripts and other records.

I never understood why Shannon Faulkner intentionally omitted information from her application and whether or not she genuinely wanted to attend the Citadel or if she simply wanted to expose gender discrimination at the state-funded institution. If she did want to expose gender discrimination—did her ends justify her means?

Her acceptance letter was later rescinded when the Citadel found out she was a woman: "You are not eligible for admission. The Citadel day program is a single-gender college program for males."[8] The Citadel later alleged that by omitting her gender, Shannon Faulkner intended to deceive them during the admissions process. If deception was part of the reason for her denial, however, the Citadel should have stated that on their letter of rescission. It was clear that the reason she was not eligible to attend the Citadel was because of her gender.

After Shannon Faulkner was notified that her admission was in error due to her gender, Faulkner sued the Citadel for violating her 14th Amendment right to equal protection under the law. The basis of the lawsuit is that single-sex education by a state-funded school is discriminatory and unconstitutional. The case became a media circus and gained national attention from many organizations such as the American Civil Liberties Union and the South Carolina Chapter of the National Organization for Women. These organizations realized the case had far-reaching implications for women's rights, especially regarding those who are excluded from state-funded institutions because of gender and because of a similar case involving the Virginia Military Institute (VMI). VMI also had a no-female policy and attempted to establish a "separate but equal" female version of VMI at Mary Baldwin College. The VMI case went before the U.S. Supreme Court, which ruled against VMI's no-female policy and forced VMI to admit female cadets, beginning in 1997.[9]

According to Shannon Faulkner's attorneys, the Citadel's defense was based on the assumption that "they did not need to provide women with a military-style education because there are not enough women who want such an education." The Citadel argued that they could justify offering a unique educational opportunity to men and not to women.

In August 1993, the district court entered a preliminary injunction, ordering that Faulkner be allowed to attend day classes at the Citadel. The district court also noted, "The defendants have failed to articulate an important policy that substantially supports offering the unique benefits of a Citadel-type education to men and not to women, and the Citadel's refusal to admit Faulkner to its Corps of Cadets because of her sex violates her constitutional rights under the Equal Protection Clause of the Fourteenth Amendment of the United States Constitution."[10]

It's interesting that in our day and age, women are still fighting for equal treatment and equality under the law. There are many laws that have been enacted to protect us as citizens; however, there are groups throughout the United States that are still fighting for equal protection under the law—especially women. Many institutions and establishments must be forced by courts of law as well as the court of public opinion when it comes to providing equal protection.

It only takes one person to make a difference and to call attention to injustice. Yet so many of us walk away because we are afraid to fight or are afraid of what speaking truth to power may do to our reputations or the effect it may have on our finances or our well-being. Many of the "misbehaving" women also knew the risks involved and many did not set out to make a name for themselves or to become heroes. They just wanted an opportunity to prove that they could excel on their own terms. Many of these women did not ask for special treatment because of their gender because they did not look at their gender as limiting. Where would many of us be today if it were not for women like Elizabeth Cady Stanton, Betty Friedan, Rosa Parks, Shirley Chisholm, and the other matriarchs of the women's and civil rights movements?

After their initial victory, Faulkner's lawyers did ask the court to excuse her from the traditional "knob" crew cut on the grounds that it would stigmatize her as a woman. The court ruled in favor of the haircut. I agree with the court. There are many instances where women seek opportunities for equality and then use their gender as a way to plead for special consideration. In some instances there are legitimate reasons that may exclude a woman from performing a job because of her gender; however, if a uniform or a haircut is part of the rules in any establishment, then compliance is necessary. Following a two-week trial during the spring of 1994, the district court found that the Citadel's males-only admissions policy violated the Equal Protection Clause and ordered the academy to admit Faulkner to the Corps of Cadets beginning in the fall of 1994. The Citadel was also ordered to plan to admit women beginning with the fall of 1995.

The ruling was a victory for Faulkner and her supporters. Her response to the ruling stated, "When I started this lawsuit, I was told I would never enter the Citadel. I'd say I'm being selfish and doing this just for me. But I do, in a way, think it's [also for the benefit of] women who might follow me."[11]

There are many times when we decide to fight for our rights or for the rights of another marginalized person or group; however, we do not always realize the far-reaching implications when attention is called to any type of injustice. When Rosa Parks decided not to give up her seat, many thought she was tired, while others thought she was disobedient; however, she sparked the Civil Rights movement. You may need to ask yourself if you are willing to be that tiny spark. There are times when the fight starts off being just about you and your own situation, but later you or others realize that its effect is greater than you could have imagined. This victory was not just about Shannon but about all the women who were allowed to attend this institution.

An appeals court later granted the Citadel a stay; however, in August 1995, the 4th Circuit and the Supreme Court refused to stop Faulkner from becoming the first female cadet in the institution's 152-year history. After the Supreme Court's decision, the Citadel actively sought to recruit female applicants, and four women entered the Corps of Cadets in August 1996. The Citadel's Board of Visitors voted to end the male-only admissions policy and to admit women to the Citadel's Corps of Cadets. The institution announced, "Effective immediately, the Citadel will enthusiastically accept qualified female applicants into the Corps of Cadets."[12]

On August 14, 1995, Faulkner was escorted onto campus by four U.S. marshals. Her private room was equipped with a dead-bolt lock and 24-hour video surveillance. She was harassed relentlessly and received numerous death threats and disparaging remarks. Her parents' home was reportedly vandalized, and bumper stickers and T-shirts referring to her by derogatory names were selling like hotcakes in South Carolina. In spite of all the controversy, Faulkner began her initial cadet training with the tradition known as "hell week"; however, after a few hours on her first day of training, Faulkner and four other cadets collapsed in the

100-degree heat. Faulkner was taken to the infirmary where she spent the remainder of her first week. The publicity she received was overwhelming because her case had gained national attention, and the media as well as her supporters and opponents followed her every move. Some speculated that her weight and physical condition were reasons for her exhaustion and inability to complete the rigorous training. It was clear that the stress along with other factors was taking a toll on Faulkner, and shortly after her historic legal victory, Faulkner voluntarily resigned as a cadet due to stress brought on by the legal battle, the immense cruelty she endured, her isolation, and physical exhaustion.

One of her lawyers characterized the environment and conditions Faulkner endured at the academy as "sanctioned hate."[13] Many of the male cadets openly celebrated her resignation on campus by hugging one another, riding mattresses across the floors, and jogging through the streets shouting derogatory remarks about Faulkner. Her decision to resign was a disappointment to many of her supporters.

Shannon Faulkner may have lost the battle, but she won the war. While she did not complete her journey at the Citadel, she paved the way for all the women who came after her. At the tender age of nineteen, she took on a battle that would eventually end 150 years of discrimination towards women that disguised itself as tradition.

There are many of us who are willing to fight for what we believe in, and many brave souls have died for their convictions. There are many times when our life, our health, and our well-being are affected by the stress and we may decide to end the fight or pass the baton. It does not mean we are quitters; it just means that during the fight we sometimes must readjust our priorities. It may also mean that we may decide that the organization is no longer one we care to be a part of, once the ugliness is revealed. In Faulkner's case, there were many instances where the fight was no longer about her but more about the agendas of many of the organizations that supported her.

According to enrollment data published by the Citadel, in May 2005, 118 women were in attendance. Faulkner now works as a middle school teacher and in a December 2009 interview with *Good Morning America*, Faulkner said, "When I think about other women being at the Citadel now and the number that graduated, that's my prize. It's not the gold ring; it's the fact that there are a couple hundred [women] that either wear it now or will wear it. Yes, [the Citadel] is not for all women, but the fact that they have that choice, that's the prize."[14]

Sarah Palin: "Only Dead Fish Go with the Flow"

> *"Americans expect us to go to Washington for the right reasons, and not just to mingle with the right people. Politics isn't just a game of clashing parties and competing interests. The right reason is to challenge the status quo, to serve the common good and to leave this nation better than we found it. No one expects us to agree on everything. But we are expected to govern with integrity, good will, clear convictions and...a servant's heart."*

Superwoman or quitter extraordinaire? Regardless of whether you are one of the millions who love her or one of the likely equal number who hate her, you cannot deny that Sarah Palin made history. Some of what she is remembered for are her notable quotes, including the subtitle of this section and others such as "Drill, baby, drill!" and, "They say the only difference between a hockey mom and a pit bull is lipstick."

Sarah Louise Heath was born in Sandpoint, Idaho, on February 11, 1964, the third of four children born to Chuck and Sally Heath. During high school she was team captain for the Wasilla High School Warriors basketball team, where she was nicknamed "Sarah

Barracuda" for her competitive nature. She also actively participated and held several positions in student government. After high school, Palin entered beauty pageants to help pay her way through college—winning many scholarships, including the coveted Ms. Wasilla in 1984. During college, she majored in journalism and later worked briefly as a sportscaster in Anchorage. After college, Palin married her high school sweetheart, Todd Palin, a commercial fisherman and part native Eskimo—together the couple has five children.[15]

By all accounts, Palin's rise to power is inspiring to women and to anyone who wants to make a difference. According to Palin,

> I was just your average hockey mom and signed up for the PTA because I wanted to make my kids' public education better. When I ran for City Council, I didn't need focus groups and voter profiles because I knew those voters, and knew their families, too. Before I became governor of the great state of Alaska, I was mayor of my hometown. I guess a small-town mayor is sort of like a "community organizer" except that you have actual responsibilities.[16]

She saw a need, she had a voice, and she did not sit back and wait for someone else to make a difference; she realized that responsibility rested on her shoulders. Palin ran for mayor of Wasilla in 1996 based on her concerns about how revenue from a new sales tax in Wasilla would be spent. She saw wasteful spending as an issue that could be used to challenge the status quo and what she dubbed as the "old boys' club." She would go on to defeat the incumbent mayor, John Stein, 651 to 440 votes. Whether or not her opponents took her seriously is anyone's guess; however, many felt that "Sarah Barracuda" took the mayoral race to a whole different level; instead of using local issues like infrastructure as the platform for her debate, she used abortion and gun-control, a tactic that was polarizing to many within the party. Polarizing or not, she was elected mayor of Wasilla.

After serving as mayor of Wasilla, she served as an ethics advisor on an oil and gas commission, but later resigned over what she called a "lack of ethics." One of the board members she reportedly exposed was also the state's GOP chairman. Palin challenged him for doing party work on the public's dime and for giving sensitive information to lobbyists.

It is clear that Palin was a force to be reckoned with—many felt that Palin's exposing corrupted officials was somewhat ballsy and even constituted political suicide; however, she continued her fight to clean up state and local government and ran for governor in 2006 on a "clean government" platform.

In spite of receiving very little support from fellow Republicans and being outspent by her Democratic opponent, she won the election and became the youngest and first woman governor of Alaska. As governor, Palin continued her fight for "clean government" and pushed for an ethics bill. She later withdrew her support for the "bridge to nowhere," a move that many saw as her claim to fame and a symbol of what was wrong with government spending policies.

Palin did not garner national recognition until she made her world debut as the vice presidential candidate of John McCain, becoming the first female vice presidential nominee of the Republican Party. Senator McCain gave Palin the nod after Hillary Clinton lost the Democratic Party nomination and was not selected by Barack Obama as his running mate. Many speculated that the reason McCain selected Palin as his running mate was to boost his support among women voters, especially those who had supported Clinton. McCain dismissed the speculation and vigorously defended his selection, stating, "Governor Palin is a tough executive who has demonstrated during her time in office that she is ready to be president. She has brought Republicans and Democrats together within her administration and has a record of delivering on the change and reform that we need in Washington."[17]

Reportedly, it never dawned on Palin that she was not qualified to be the Vice President of the United States. She felt that she was more than equipped and did not know why her opponents felt otherwise. I often wonder if Palin would have faced the same scrutiny if her name was Samuel Palin. Although there was a lot of media attention when former president George H. W. Bush nominated Dan Quayle for his vice presidential candidate, I don't believe he suffered the same humiliation and intense questioning Palin did.

According to Palin, she was not surprised when she received the call:

> When I got the call, it was not such a shocking call to me. I felt quite confident in my abilities and my executive experience and I knew that this is an executive, administrative job. I was happy to get in there and contribute.[18]

No one can deny the impact Palin had on her party, which was divided prior to McCain's nomination based on extreme views within the Republican party; however, when McCain introduced Pain, she energized the base with her debut and her speech at the Republican National Convention. One reason she received high approval from traditional Republicans was because of her anti-gay and anti-abortion position, as well as her family values.

Not everyone embraced her stance on family values, however, in light of the fact that Palin's seventeen-year-old daughter was pregnant and unmarried. Many perceived her as a hypocrite; however, Palin maintained that hers was the all-American family.

Many parents are keenly aware that though we may raise our children well and to the best of our ability, our children may not always adhere to what we teach them, often bowing to peer and other types of pressure. That does not mean we are not good parents. It has been my own experience as a child and even as a parent that experience is the best teacher.

During the campaign, Palin lost support among women, many of whom felt she was not qualified for the position. Some believed she gave women a bad name, reminding many of women who became successful because of their looks and not their brains. She was not the type of person most women would choose to represent them. There is nothing wrong with being attractive; however, the high level of public service to which Palin aspired required more than beauty—it required the intellectual capacity to effectively represent and lead the masses. It required someone who could unite and not divide the country. Without the ability to convince a majority of the electorate, no person, male or female, is qualified to hold the second highest office in the nation—a heartbeat away from the presidency, as the saying goes.

On the other hand, some women were fascinated with Palin's image as the "super-woman": those women who appear to have it all and manage with grace in spite of the odds. In addition to being the governor of Alaska, Palin was a wife and mother of five children, including a special-needs child. The McCain campaign appeared to be banking on the fact that Palin would appeal to the many women who juggled family responsibilities while also holding down a full-time job. Though she was presented as a "woman who has it all," she received very little support from the women's movement.

Many women are instinctively supportive of female candidates because women have very little representation in the House and Senate. Many women also want a woman to shatter the ultimate glass ceiling by assuming the highest position in the country, President of the United States. As the campaign went on, some women reported that they felt if they supported Ms. Palin, they were sending the wrong message as they strongly believed she was not qualified. Adding fuel to the fire was Palin's mangled speech and lack of knowledge on political issues around the world, which provided the monologue for many late night shows. After all, she tried to convince Katie Couric that she was prepared to deal with foreign policy because of Russia's proximity to Alaska.

All throughout the campaign, Palin was criticized for everything from what she wore to how many times she paraded her kids (including a baby with Down syndrome and an unwed, pregnant teen daughter) on the campaign trail. I strongly felt that this was a double standard; I have not seen a candidate running for office who has not used his or her family in some type of campaign rally or a photo op, from the Obama girls to the Bush twins as well as Chelsea Clinton. Seriously, if "Samuel" Palin had paraded his kids on the campaign trail, would he have received the same scrutiny? I seriously doubt it because his wife would have been home or nearby, tending to the needs of the children.

Sarah responded to her critics by saying, "It never occurred to me that I couldn't do the job because of children. My children are my strength ... They allow me to be grounded."[19]

The McCain-Palin ticket went on to lose their bid for the president/vice president of the United States. Many put the blame on McCain's selection of Palin; however, the country was in the throes of change and wanted a different party in the White House. I doubt McCain would have won even if he had selected another candidate as his running mate.

Less than a year after the presidential campaign, Palin announced that she was resigning as the governor of Alaska. According to Palin,

> I resigned as governor of Alaska because I wasn't going to run for a second term, and I was heading into a lame duck term. We came back to a new normal in Alaska. Everything had so changed in my administration. There were so many opposition researchers up there in Alaska that were sent, probably, by the Obama camp.... It was a point where my state of Alaska was being hampered by my presence there [as governor].[20]

Her announcement shocked her opponents as well as her

supporters. After all, this was her first term in office and she still had about eighteen months left to serve the state of Alaska. Many suspected she had not stated the real reason she was quitting; some speculated that it was due to the many ethics violations she was accused of, while others felt that it was more about her finances. During her resignation speech, she cited media attacks on her family as one of the reasons for her resignation. However, many did not believe she resigned due to media attacks, given the way Palin had put her family on display and often talked about them during her speeches.

Palin stated that she felt she could serve her state and her country more effectively on issues that were important to her—energy independence and national security, for example—if she were not the governor. Still, her resignation led many to view her as a quitter. Others suggested the resignation would afford her more time to prepare for the 2012 election, or that she believed she could make more money if she were not the governor.

In many political circles, her decision was not seen as presidential, and many speculated that her decision would hurt her political future. In spite of all her mishaps and blunders, the country still seemed unable to get enough of Sarah Palin. She has been described as a lightning rod for criticism, yet on occasion she has made the criticism work to her advantage.

In her book, *Going Rogue: An American Life*, Palin describes how she was treated by the McCain camp. Palin states that her family, friends, and political associates were under strict instructions not to talk to the media. Her description sounds as if she was at a concentration camp rather than a presidential campaign. "Never before had I been involved in a campaign that placed such an emphasis on packaging."[21] She was also upset at the way communication about her daughter's pregnancy was handled. The campaign allegedly disseminated a press release on the situation that Palin had not seen or approved. "If [the managers of the campaign] weren't going to let me speak my heart and mind even about an intimate issue affecting my own family, what would they let me speak to?"[21]

Why was Sarah Palin treated as a puppet? Was it because she was a woman, or because the McCain campaign feared she would do more harm than good if she were allowed to be herself? Who vetted her as a candidate, after all? Was her experience—or lack of it—an unknown prior to her selection? If her inexperience with global politics was a liability for the campaign, why was that not taken into consideration before she was invited to join the ticket?

Ms. Palin's supporters felt that the media treated her poorly; however, when a person is running for national office, media scrutiny and even criticism are inevitable. Clearly, not everyone saw Sarah Palin as the media darling. However, that is the price to be paid when one aspires to public service or celebrity status for any reason. Is it the media's fault if Palin performed poorly during the interview with Katie Couric or at the vice presidential debate?

I should state clearly that I do not subscribe to Palin's political philosophy; however, I admire her for several reasons. First, she refuses to let anyone define her or her views, even when they are unpopular. She knew that quitting her job before she completed her term would hurt her political future; however, she made her decision in spite of the advisors who counseled against resignation. Sarah Palin marches to the beat of her own drum, and does not care whom the beat pleases, other than herself and her family. Could this be why she continues to be so fascinating?

Even after her electoral defeat and resignation, why do millions still love Sarah Palin? Her uniqueness and unpredictability make her appealing to many. Is she, in some unexpected way, a symbol for twenty-first–century feminism, or can she perhaps be considered an accidental feminist? After all, she took on the old boys' network when many tried to define her by telling her what to say, what to wear, and when to speak. She has been brutally honest about her decision to carry a child to term even while knowing that the child would have Down syndrome. She works outside the home though she is a wife and mother.

Many women in corporate America struggle daily with important decisions as we juggle family responsibilities and our careers. We feel guilty about not spending enough time with our families, wishing we had the means to stay at home and still live our dreams. Few of us are brave enough to challenge conventional wisdom and refuse to let other people define us. Palin was called a quitter for not finishing out the remainder of her term, and while I understand that she was elected to serve the citizens of Alaska, does that mean she should have stayed in a job in which she felt she could no longer serve her constituents effectively? The citizens of Alaska deserve a governor who can serve effectively and without distractions.

How many of us have started a job that took a toll on our health or our families, a job to which our hearts were no longer committed? Deep down, we knew that we were no longer engaged and as a result, we could no longer be or were no longer effective. Most of us who struggled with this difficult decision did not face the sort of public scrutiny and criticism that was leveled at Sarah Palin. Why the different standard?

While it is true that she was a public figure who chose to put her life on display by running for public office, we ought to remember that she is also someone's mother, daughter, sister, wife, and friend. She is also a human being and deserves to be respected in spite of her political philosophy. Public persecution of women by women is not what the matriarchs of the women's movement envisioned for us. As women, we are still fighting for equality and we need the support of each other—we do not need to be tearing each other down because we share different beliefs or political philosophies.

A woman of great faith, Palin has also relied on her faith when faced with many difficult and personal decisions. She has been very open and honest regarding her decision to have her fifth child after tests revealed early in the pregnancy that her child would be born with Down syndrome. She is pro-life, and her faith and trust in God sustained her to the point where she did not ever consider ending the pregnancy. According to Sarah,

> Trig is beautiful and already adored by us. We knew through early testing he would face special challenges, and we feel privileged that God would entrust us with this gift and allow us unspeakable joy as he entered our lives. We have faith that every baby is created for good purpose and has potential to make this world a better place. We are truly blessed.[22]

She was faced with a very personal decision and could have easily chosen another path; however, with faith and much prayer, she made the decision that was best for her and has inspired many women who have struggled with the decision as to whether they should bring a special needs child into the world.

Sarah knows who she is and Whose she is:

> I do know there is a God. My life is in His hands. I encourage readers to do what I did many years ago, invite Him in to take over … then see what He will do and how He will get you through. Test Him on this. You'll see there's no such thing as coincidence.[23]

I hope that we can take a page from Palin's book and live out our dreams, realizing that life is about choices. Many times in my career, and especially after my separation from my last employer, I questioned and reflected on my decisions about whether to take a stand or to go along and get along. Sarah Palin's quote from her resignation speech, "Only dead fish go with the flow," echoed in my mind many times as I resolved to the best of my ability to chart my own course, rather than allow others to do it for me.

Hillary Clinton: Redefining the Possibilities of Women in Government

> *"I suppose I could have stayed home and baked cookies and had teas, but what I decided to do was to fulfill my profession, which I entered before my husband was in public life."*

From the time Hillary Rodham attracted national attention for being the first student commencement speaker at Wellesley College, it was clear to all who knew her that she was, indeed, intent upon pursing a life of influence in the public arena. And from the time she stepped upon the national stage as First Lady, it was clear that she would not be content with being a social decoration for her husband's presidency. Her staunch advocacy of an ambitious national healthcare plan, though not bearing direct fruit during President Clinton's term in office, in many ways laid the groundwork for later success in this area by President Barack Obama. It is still open to debate whether women have truly shattered the glass ceiling, but Hillary Rodham Clinton has certainly made a number of sizable fissures.

During the 1992 presidential campaign for her husband, Hillary Clinton came under fire for comments made about her role and responsibilities if she became the First Lady. At the time of the campaign, she had an absorbing career outside the home as attorney and partner in an Arkansas law firm. She was also a children's advocate. In the spring of 1992, following criticism about the propriety of working for a law firm that received contracts from a state where her husband was governor, Hillary responded with the quote cited at the beginning of this section. Her comments were viewed as condescending and belittling to women who chose to stay at home rather than pursue careers in the workplace. However, other women, who were trying to balance their own careers while taking care of their families, saw her comments as liberating.

Deciding whether to work in the home raising a family or to

have a career outside the home while raising a family is a decision that has been hotly debated by women for decades. This choice is not an easy one for the millions of working women who struggle to put food on the table and would love the opportunity to be stay-at-home moms who spend more time raising their families. There are other women who can afford to stay home; however, they choose to follow their passion, which involves working outside of the home. Many of these women believe you can have it all.

There are some mothers who welcome the opportunity to be away from their children for a small amount of time because they feel it's healthy to get a break away from their kids.

As I look at the various alternatives facing women today, who am I to judge? I am happy that women have choices and are free to follow the path that leads them to self-fulfillment. Hillary has been criticized for always being scripted and choosing the politically correct route when it comes to many important decisions; however, in the above situation, I admire her for being true to herself.

She pushed the role of First Lady far beyond the largely ceremonial and social functions carried out by many of her predecessors. Many in the public were first astonished, then intimidated, then hostile, as they watched the president's spouse actually undertaking a substantive policy initiative with potentially far-reaching ramifications. There were a lot of questions regarding Hillary's qualifications and experience mainly because she did not always publicize her accomplishments and chose to work in the background; however, she set about the task of taking on some of the most entrenched and intractable social issues facing Americans. She spearheaded statewide educational reform in Arkansas and was later appointed by her husband to lead the Task Force on National Healthcare Reform. Undeterred by the criticism her ideas received, she continued to advocate, lecture, and stump for National Healthcare Reform—even though she had to wear a bulletproof vest at times—until prolonged congressional inaction finally killed momentum for the plan in 1994.

Even with this defeat, she didn't surrender her initiative, and I find that admirable. There are many times when we experience defeat and setbacks that threaten our careers and dampen our spirits. Although we did not set out to fail and failure was never an option—we failed nonetheless. What do we do? Where do we go? What options do we have? We should all get up, dust ourselves off, and either try again or move on to other endeavors. We need to learn from our mistakes. We may cry a bit and choose to drown out our sorrows by having a drink. We may cope by going for a drive, exercising, or spending time with family and friends whose goals are to either help us forget or help us cope. In whatever way we adapt, we have to move forward. We cannot let situations or circumstances control our lives. We have to learn from our mistakes—after all, experience is the best teacher. We use it to guide us going forward.

Hillary could have thrown in the towel and given up in the face of defeat but she kept marching on—she went on to lead the efforts to enact the State Children's Health Insurance Program in 1997, fought to increase funding for research on childhood asthma and prostate cancer at the National Institutes of Health, helped focus public and policy attention on what would become known as Gulf War Syndrome, and helped create, along with Attorney General Janet Reno, the Justice Department's Office on Violence against Women. However, she would later say that her proudest achievement as First Lady was the passage of the Adoption and Safe Families Act. Clearly, the defeat of her healthcare initiative did little to dim Hillary's determination to push for policies that would improve the lives of children and families.

With the retirement announcement of Daniel Patrick Moynihan, long-time senator from New York, Hillary's name soon became associated with the possibility of a run for the Senate. Almost as soon as the buzz started, her potential candidacy was decried as carpetbagging and political opportunism at its worst. Many gave her little chance of success, but after establishing residency in

New York and conducting "listening tours" to every county in the state, and after slugging it out in a campaign that would generate a record total of $90 million in campaign expense, Clinton came out the victor. Once in the Senate, she continued her determined course of leadership and advocacy for issues that she believed in. She would win reelection in 2006. Whether or not Hillary had ambitions of becoming the president of the United States at that point in her career is anyone's guess; however, she had a successful career and many supporters wanted her to accomplish what no woman in U.S. history had accomplished—the presidency of the United States. As her supporters became more vocal, Hillary seriously considered her options.

As the election year of 2008 approached, she would embark on her most ambitious effort yet. In this same year, she and Sarah Palin would both become players in the presidential election; many female supporters of both candidates hoped either Clinton or Palin would become either the first female vice president or president. Of course, it would be difficult to imagine two individuals who were farther apart on the political spectrum. Therein lies a lesson, perhaps: women, like any other demographic group, cannot be easily categorized as to their political beliefs. We don't have to be all Democrats, Republicans, religious, feminist, or any other single political or social profile to support one another. Although we are different, we share many of the same struggles.

Both Clinton and Palin, ultimately, were unsuccessful in their quests in 2008. During her campaign, Clinton lost the support of some blacks who initially supported her but felt her campaign was unduly divisive. Categorizing one historically marginalized group as more downtrodden than another was viewed as both politically and socially irresponsible. On the other hand, as noted above, many felt that McCain's choice of Palin was a desperate and shallow attempt to gain women voters who had supported Clinton and were disillusioned by her defeat at the hands of Barack Obama.

Events seemed to indicate, however, that while women voters

felt that it would have been historically important to have a woman as president or vice president, they still wanted a candidate, whether male or female, who was qualified to lead and who represented their issues. They were not ready to vote for Palin simply because Hillary lost the nomination. And so, in the end, both these historic efforts involving women fell short of their ultimate goals.

I deeply admire Clinton for her determination to hold onto her goals despite vicious opposition and even threats of violence. Before and after the campaign, many felt she should wear more dresses and skirts as a way to look feminine and show her softer side; however, she did not bow to the pressure and stayed true to herself even if it meant wearing mostly pantsuits and whatever else made her comfortable. She stands for what she believes in, even at the risk of being perceived as a polarizing figure or a domineering, calculating politician. Whether leading education reform in Arkansas, spearheading the difficult effort toward healthcare reform as First Lady, running for a hotly contested Senate seat in New York, or serving as Secretary of State on the tumultuous world stage in the administration of the person who defeated her presidential aspirations, Hillary Clinton has proven that she is determined to lead the way and determined to follow a course of her own choosing.

Also a woman of great faith, Hillary has relied on her faith to take her through some of the deepest, darkest times in her life. In her autobiography *Living History*, she describes her faith as a "crucial, though deeply personal, part of my life and my family's life."[24] It's hard to imagine the embarrassment she must have felt after learning of her husband's indiscretions with Monica Lewinsky. It's also difficult to contemplate the effect of the many vicious attacks she's encountered throughout her life; however, she endured—and relied on her faith—the same faith that was instilled in her as a child—to help her to cope as well as forgive.

According to Hillary, "I've been tested in ways that are both publicly known and those that are not so well known or not known at all."[25] There are times in our lives when we feel like the world as we know it has collapsed around us and nothing seems to make sense—we feel like closing our eyes and giving up because we don't want to deal with the pain and suffering we are feeling; however, we call on God to have him strengthen and comfort us as well as provide answers—these are the times when we rely on our faith and we pray for wisdom to understand what we are going through. Hillary relied on "her personal faith and the prayers of others sustain her." Her faith has been tested, and she believes, "those moments in time when you are tested, it is absolutely essential that you be grounded in your faith. I am very grateful that I had a grounding in faith that gave me the courage and the strength to do what I thought was right, regardless of what the world thought. I'm not sure I would have gotten through it without my faith."[26]

Mae West: Breaking All the Rules

> *"When I am good, I am very good. But when I am bad, I am better."*

It is hard to deny the impact that the media has on our society, especially in the information technology era where even a home video can "go viral." The media has had a huge impact on women and the way women are portrayed or presented. Known for bringing us the stories that we care about deeply through awareness or by sensationalizing other issues in which we have very little interest or feel very strongly about, the media has changed the way we view the world.

From the silent era of film to the present, women have fought for their place in front of and behind the camera, and such is the case with Mae West. Early in the history of film, the roles of women were mostly limited to acting or perhaps costume design; more recently, however, women are winning respect—and awards—as screenwriters, directors, producers, and studio executives.

We have a love-hate relationship with the media depending on who or what is being covered. For decades—if not longer—women's ideas of themselves have been shaped by the media, and in the twentieth and twenty-first centuries, movies, television, advertising, magazines, the Internet, and music have been factors in defining femininity.

According to Susan J. Douglas, "Along with our parents—and sometimes more influential than our parents—the mass media raised us, socialized us, entertained us, comforted us, deceived us, disciplined us, told us what we could do and told us what we couldn't."[27]

The media has been a partner in women's fight for equality under the law and in society. From the earliest days of first-wave feminism in the late 1800s, women have relied on the media to help publicize and advance their various causes. In addition to word of mouth, early feminist leaders relied on posters, pamphlets, newspapers, and other printed media to advance the movement.

With the birth of cinema, women had yet another media outlet available for the shaping and dissemination of the feminine image. As already mentioned, in the earliest days, the majority of women in the budding industry were the actresses, and the images of them that were projected onto the flickering screen were generally those of weak, gullible, trusting, charming beings who needed to be rescued from death—or worse—by a strong, virile, resourceful, decisive man.

By the 1920s, Hollywood and the motion picture industry had acquired an unsavory reputation, brought vividly to public attention by several scandals. The result was the formation of the Motion Picture Producers and Distributors Association, the predecessor organization of the Motion Picture Association of America (MPAA), and the first morality clause for the industry, commonly known as the Hays Code.

In his book, *Complicated Women: Sex and Power in Pre-Code Hollywood*, Mick LaSalle described women in film during the pre–Hays Code days:

> Before the Code, women on the screen took lovers,

> had babies out of wedlock, got rid of cheating husbands, enjoyed their sexuality, held down professional positions without apologizing for their self-sufficiency, and in general acted the way many of us think women only acted after 1968. [28]

Pre–Hays Code was a time of unusual freedom and discovery for women in film. Women struggled to be recognized for their talents, wanting to be portrayed in ways that were true to themselves, regardless of whether they received favorable or unfavorable reviews from the public or critics.

Actresses like Mae West expressed sexual freedom on the silver screen at a time when women were not generally permitted to be sexual beings in the public sphere. The "moral majority" generally disapproved of such female independence, blamed by some on women receiving the vote in 1920. During this period many felt anxiety over women's new place in society. Thus, the increasingly sensual portrayal of women in the movies angered many and the call for government censorship became louder. Vote or no vote, independence or liberalism notwithstanding, women's modernization or not, the public was not fully prepared to view women as vamps or vixens.

Born Mary Jane West on August 17, 1893, in Brooklyn, New York, Mae West as she was affectionately called began her career as a young child in Vaudeville. She was the oldest of three children born to working class parents. Her parents recognized she was talented at a young age; however, they wanted her to follow a more traditional career path such as a seamstress or garment worker. Instead of discipline when many family members thought she was acting out, her mother reportedly encouraged her individuality and was probably responsible for Mae's larger than life personality. When Mae began impersonating family members and friends at a young age, her parents could no longer deny that Mae had a special gift. Her mother began taking her to see plays and Vaudeville performances and her love for the arts grew. She reportedly imagined herself performing on the stage before packed audiences. These performances influenced Mae's career and she would later credit performers and entertainers like Bert Williams for helping her to become a great performer.

At the tender age of five she began performing for the public locally—although her father was apprehensive about having his little girl perform for the public, he later became one of her biggest supporters. Her mother further supported her talents by enrolling her in dance school at the age of seven. She began growing as a performer and before long she was winning prizes in talent competitions and appearing at local burlesque theaters. At the age of fourteen, she began her professional career as a Vaudeville performer. Many felt her impersonation of adult burlesque performers in many of her performances was too sexual for a teenager.

Mae was one of the first stars—and almost certainly the first woman—to portray sex as "something to be enjoyed openly and without shame."[29] According to reports, "at one point in her career, West was the highest paid woman in the United States." She starred in and wrote at least two films in 1933, *She Done Him Wrong*, based on her outstandingly successful stage play *Diamond Lil*, and *I'm No Angel,* which were credited with saving Paramount Pictures from impending bankruptcy.[30]

Her erotically charged performances were too sexual for the general taste, and movies like *I'm No Angel generated louder calls for censorship from many quarters.* In spite of the controversy surrounding her performances and calls for censorship, West had a successful career and continued to use her sexuality to showcase her talents. She could have chosen a different path; however, she was comfortable in her own skin, even when it meant being arrested and censored.

Although West expressed her sexual freedom on the stage and on the silver screen, she kept her personal life private—she cared about her image and did not want to be perceived as promiscuous.

West was rumored to use her marriage in 1911 to Frank Wallace, a fellow Vaudeville performer, as a cover to protect her image. She never lived with Wallace and her living arrangements further fueled the rumors that the marriage was only intended as a cover in the event "the sexually active West should become pregnant."[31] The hush-hush arrangement came to light in the 1930s, when West was at the height of her fame as an actress, playwright, and novelist. After issuing a series of denials, West finally divorced Wallace. She never remarried, though she did reportedly maintain a longstanding relationship with Paul Novak, whom she met in the 1950s. Novak moved into her home and for years was passed off as her "butler, bodyguard, and chauffeur." To avoid compromising her public image as a free spirit, the true nature of their relationship was kept quiet. However, Novak stayed with West for the rest of her life, caring for her until her death in 1980.[32]

West, in defiance of the effects of time, continued to see herself as sexually desirable well into the time in life when many women no longer concern themselves with such matters. Rather than conform to society's expectations of how a woman of "her age" should behave and present herself, West, in unexpected ways, did her part to subvert public stereotypes of women as innocent, diffident, unimaginatively virtuous beings in need of constant male supervision and protection. By constantly pushing the envelope and displaying open acceptance and even enjoyment of her sexuality, she helped open the way for women to be viewed in all the diversity and variability encompassed by the feminine experience. Rather than be limited by public disapproval or the castigation of critics, she embraced the personal meaning of her own femininity and used it to go precisely where she wished.

Indira Gandhi: Controversy, Diversity, and a Woman in the Lead

"The power to question is the basis of all human progress."

In another continent and decades before Clinton and Palin ran, respectively, for the Democratic presidential nomination and for vice president of the United States, Indira Gandhi became the first female prime minister of India. She held the position for three consecutive terms, from 1966 to 1977, and again for a fourth term from 1980 to 1984. Politics was in her blood as she was born into and grew up in a family of politicians. Her grandfather, Motilal Nehru, was an Indian nationalist leader, and her father, Jawaharlal Nehru, was the first prime minister of an independent India. She is not related to Mahatma Gandhi, the legendary figure in India's struggle for independence, but had the name because of her marriage to Feroze Gandhi.

Her early and formative years have been described as painfully lonely. Her parents were frequently taken off to jail because of their political organizing activities, and the police were no strangers to the Gandhi home as it was often used as a headquarters for the freedom struggle. According to Gandhi,

> My public life started at the age of three. I have no recollection of games, children's parties, or playing with other children. My favorite occupation as a very small child was to deliver thunderous speeches to the servants, standing on a high table. All my games were political ones; – I was, like Joan of Arc, perpetually being burned at the stake.
>
> I was very headstrong. The whole house was always in a state of tension, so that nobody had a normal life. There were police raids, arrests, and so on, [increasing] the physical and mental strain. And all the time it was in public.[33]

As I reflect on her stolen childhood, I feel a sense of sadness for Gandhi. I understand India's fight for independence during that era but wonder if she would have chosen a life of politics if she had not been born into an influential political family.

After India's attainment of independence, Gandhi's father became the prime minister of India, and after her mother lost her battle with cancer, Gandhi was responsible for managing the official residence of her father and accompanying him on his frequent foreign trips.

Her rise to power and her political aspirations became clearer after she graduated from Visva-Bharati University, Bengal, and completed her studies at Somerville College, Oxford University. She loved her country and by all indications wanted to see India's continued progress.

It is important to note the relationship she had with her father, who inspired and encouraged her. Although he placed a lot of responsibility on his daughter as a child and she in essence lost her childhood, he taught her that she could be anything she wanted to be. He did not tell her that she could not fight for her country because she was a woman or to focus on assuming traditional roles. Instead, all her life she was groomed to be a political leader, and her gender was not a factor. During a period in her career that resulted in a national state of emergency, Gandhi was heavily criticized and responded by saying:

> Every position has advantages and disadvantages. I had an advantage because of the education my father gave me and the opportunities of meeting some great people: not only politicians, but also writers, artists, and so on.[34]

This is interesting, as women's rights is a hot topic issue in India today. It is important for fathers to encourage their daughters to pursue their dreams in spite of the odds and the statistics about women in leadership. In twenty-first–century America, women are still fighting for their place at the table even though the workforce is made up of more than fifty percent women. There are several factors that play into the fight for equality, but I believe the fight starts at home in how we teach our sons and daughters to respect and view each other.

Gandhi did not shun the traditional roles of women and felt that her marriage to Feroze in 1938 fueled her political passions. During their political rise, both Feroze and Indira were arrested by the British on charges of subversion and spent thirteen months in prison.

She understood the pressures being placed on women, especially in politics. "In politics [a woman] has to work doubly hard to show one is not merely a daughter but is also a person in her own right.... Of course, being a woman, you have to work twice as hard as a man."[35] Many women today still share the sentiment that women have to work twice as hard as a man in order to be recognized as a credible player, especially in corporate America.

Prior to becoming prime minister, Gandhi held many positions and many offices. In 1959, she was elected president of the Indian National Congress and became the fourth woman in Indian history to hold this position. In 1964 she was appointed minister of information by Prime Minister Lal Bahadur Shastri and was responsible for promoting family planning—one of the most controversial topics in India due to political and religious reasons. She was not afraid of controversy and embraced the task at hand even though she knew she was putting her life at risk and possibly committing political suicide.

She became prime minister of India after Shastri's death in 1966 and held the position until India's next election in 1967. During the 1967 elections, she ran for and won election as prime minister in her own right: the first woman in history elected to lead a democracy.

During her tenure, Gandhi presided over the world's most populous democracy, a nation of 700 million people—almost bewildering in its religious, ethnic, linguistic, and cultural diversity. She implemented a voluntary sterilization program that drew heavy criticism from her opponents. To add fuel to the fire, she ordered the arrests of the main opposition leaders. She felt this was a good move as her opponents' criticism was limiting India's progress and she could not let that happen on her watch.

In 1975, she was convicted of corruption and banned from holding office for six years. She responded by refusing to resign and declared a national state of emergency, an intensely controversial situation that lasted for nearly two years. As a result of her stance and position on some of India's most controversial issues, she was voted out of office in 1977. This is a teachable moment for those of us who face different types of opposition: we have to continue the fight, but the end cannot justify the means. Having her opponents arrested was not a good move for her as Gandhi, of all persons, should have understood the importance of democracy as she witnessed India's fight for independence. Her tactics were compared to the same tactics the British used as part of India's oppression.

During my career, I have witnessed situations where a formerly marginalized group or person got into a position of power, and the oppressed became the oppressor. As an African American man, one of my former bosses should have understood the struggle of those who fought for civil rights so he could enjoy many of the freedoms he now has; however, when he got in a position of power, instead of trying to liberate others, he engaged in the same repressive behaviors he had experienced during his life. He felt that this was the type of behavior his superiors expected.

I remembered during one of our discussions when I confronted him about his biases and double-standards, he responded by saying, "It's like this: Remember how your parents used to say, 'Either I make you cry or the white man makes you cry—because if the white man makes you cry, it will hurt a lot more'?" In other words, he claimed that his intimidating treatment of certain people was actually intended to make them stronger, to hold them to a higher standard. Fear and intimidation do not equate to leadership and do not generate respect—only more fear and intimidation. Those in leadership positions should use their positions to effect great and positive change.

Having said all that, it's easy to pass judgment and play Monday morning quarterback with someone else's decisions. I am not sure why Gandhi made some of the choices she did; however, she paid the ultimate price—she lost the highest office in her country. Was she an easier target because she was a woman? There are no indications that her gender played any role in losing the elections. Some felt that she did not accomplish all the promises on her ambitious agenda—her administration made limited progress on issues such as overpopulation, hunger, limitations imposed by the caste system, inadequate sanitation, and chronic religious strife among the majority Hindus, Muslims, and other sects. She did however, lead her nation during the conflict with Pakistan and as a result, Bangladesh was created. She was also in office during India's first successful launch of a space satellite. These were some of her proudest accomplishments; however, her administration was often embroiled in controversy as a result of many of her decisions, thus overshadowing some of her great work.

Gandhi could have easily taken a back seat in India's politics as a result of the opposition she faced and being embroiled in controversy; however, she had a mission and was willing to die to accomplish her mission because she believed it would benefit her beloved India. In 1979, she returned to power and led India to become one of the fastest growing economies in the world.

She endured several threats and countless insults but stood her ground, as she felt that the controversial issues were important challenges for India and needed to be addressed.

In 1984, responding to escalating riots and growing rebellion by Sikh separatists, she made what may have been her most controversial move by ordering Indian troops to storm the Golden Temple in Amritsar—the holiest shrine of the Sikh religion. The troops were ordered to kill or capture the Sikh separatists who were said to be amassing weapons within the temple. After several long hours of fierce fighting between militant Sikhs and the soldiers, it was reported that the temple looked like a battlefield, with bodies strewn all over the complex. According to official government figures, about 600 people were killed in the raid on the temple, including the Sikh leader. Other reports placed the figure as high as 1,200.

This act caused outrage across the country and resulted in rioting among Sikhs that was countered by anti-Sikh violence. On October 31, 1984, Gandhi was assassinated by her Sikh bodyguards in an act widely seen as vengeance for the storming of the Golden Temple.

It is true that her actions as a leader are open to criticism; she clearly made some decisions that displeased many—some that could even be criticized on humanitarian grounds. Nevertheless, her life provides yet another example of a woman who was not afraid to choose the path less traveled—at least, for a woman. In a society heavily dominated by men, she rose to become the unquestioned leader of her nation, and she proved that she was more than capable of taking decisive action to protect the national interests that she believed in—even if those actions were viewed with strong disapproval or even dismay by observers. Certainly, no one could question Gandhi's mental toughness or her willingness to risk everything—even her reputation—for what mattered most to her. As the first woman elected to lead a democracy, and as head of the most populous and perhaps the most diverse democracy on the planet, she was truly a trailblazer among women. History should not overlook her shortcomings, but it should, in all fairness, view them in light of her amazing achievements.

Margaret Thatcher: Britain's "Iron Lady"

> *"People think that at the top there isn't much room. They tend to think of it as an Everest. My message is that there is tons of room at the top."*

The first female prime minister of Great Britain and the first woman to become the head of a modern European government was Margaret Thatcher. A highly respected world leader renowned for her tough leadership style, Margaret Thatcher earned the title "the Iron Lady." Her conservative political philosophy represented a major departure from the previously liberal policies that had been dominant in British government for decades. During her time as prime minister, she presided over a successful war in the Falklands, reduced the power of trade unions, and weathered two major recessions in the United Kingdom.

Born Margaret Roberts in October 1925 in Grantham, England, to working-class parents, she was born at a time when Grantham was still recovering from the effects of the Great War of 1914–18. As a result of the war, many of her neighbors were poor and often struggled to put food on the table. Her father was a successful grocer who later became the mayor of Grantham. It is not clear at what age Margaret's love of politics became apparent—maybe it came from her father. However, she did not initially pursue law or politics in college. She applied for and won a scholarship to attend Somerville College of Oxford University where she studied natural science with a concentration in chemistry and earned her bachelor's degree. She later attended Oxford University where she received her master of arts degree. She also studied to become a barrister but not before a brief career as a research chemist. In 1951 she married Denis Thatcher, a successful businessman, and had two children. After taking time off to raise her children, she rose to power by holding various positions in the Conservative Party.

After the defeat of the Conservative Party in 1964, Thatcher was appointed as the spokesperson for the opposition on pensions and national insurance. She also held opposition posts on housing, treasury, fuel and power, transport, and education. Following the Conservative victory in 1970, Edward Heath appointed her as the education secretary. In this role, she faced opposition because at this time, student radicalism was at an all-time high. Although her speeches were often disrupted by protesters and her opponents did not make it easy for her to do her job or to accomplish her agenda, yet she endured. She generated a storm of controversy by bringing an end to free school milk for children over seven and for increasing school meal charges. This move earned her the title, "Margaret Thatcher the Milk Snatcher." Being thus vilified and criticized could have forced her to lose focus. Instead, she used the attacks and negativity to motivate her and strengthen her resolve.

Being in politics or other public positions is not for the weak of heart. Imagine having your life exposed before the world: what you wear, how you look, and everything in between. I am not aware of anyone who went into politics because of the glitz and glamour. Being vilified for your beliefs and risking your life for the greater good is often met by opposition instead of approval, yet the number of candidates throwing their hats into the ring has not lessened. The children of these families are often exposed to a kind of scrutiny they never imagined because of the decisions of their parents. I often wondered how Chelsea Clinton and Bristol Palin felt about the disparaging remarks made about them and if they resented their parents as a result. Consider the cost! Maybe Thatcher drew her strength from having a father who was a political figure and understood the attacks her father received; however, she also saw the big picture.

When the Conservative Party lost a second general election in October 1974, Thatcher ran against Heath for the leadership. This was a very calculated and risky move; however, to everyone's surprise including her own, she defeated him.

This is a lesson for many of us who are crippled by fear or are afraid to challenge the status quo. Many saw Edward Heath as being ineffective, including those in his own party—yet they chose not to openly oppose or challenge him. However, Thatcher's vision for the Conservative Party allowed her to challenge the status quo.

Challenging the status quo almost always placed me in the line of fire; it would have been easier if I just acquiesced and followed the leader, even knowing that my leader was not leading me down the paths of righteousness. I always asked questions to achieve clarity, and my questioning was not always received graciously.

Whether or not Thatcher's challenge to the status quo was risky, a gamble, calculated, or seen at the time as politically expedient—it paid off, as the Conservative Party went on to win the general election, making Margaret Thatcher Britain's first-ever woman prime minister. As prime minister, she was determined to return Great Britain to greatness and reverse many of the policies that she viewed as being responsible for the country's decline.

She took on many establishments, including the powerful trade unions, which she saw as standing in the way of national progress. Her leadership style and willingness to challenge her critics, even if they were world leaders, earned her the title of the "Iron Lady" from the Soviets, which she later adopted as a way of setting the tone for her leadership style.

She led the Conservative Party to three consecutive victories in three general elections (1979, 1983 and 1987)—the first British prime minister in the twentieth century to do so.

Heavily criticized for her many policies or lack thereof, some were surprised at the strong criticism she faced from women, despite having achieved what only a few women in the world achieved. Like Golda Meir, however, Thatcher has been faulted for not using her position to help women and for not recognizing that the feminist movement was even partially responsible for her success.

She remains one of the most controversial figures in Britain's history. Her critics believed that her economic policies—many of which were viewed as harsh or uncaring—were also a source of social division in Great Britain, particularly in the way they undermined many of the institutions of British social welfare. However, Thatcher's proponents cite her leadership as a factor in transforming the British economy.

There is no disagreement, however, on the fact that her time as prime minister brought fundamental, historic changes to Great

Britain, or on the fact that with her tough stance on the policies in which she believed, Thatcher often compelled the respect of even those who were among her most entrenched critics. She is often credited with fundamentally shifting the terms of the political and social debate in Great Britain; indeed, the leadership of the opposition Labour Party was forced to change by the end of her term; the "New Labour" stance of Tony Blair would never have developed without the presence of the Thatcher government.

She was widely seen as a political and philosophical ally of Ronald Reagan, and, indeed, these two leaders, on either side of the Atlantic, both opposed labor unions, both favored privatization of industry, both worked for smaller government, and both pushed for tax reduction.

Thatcher's right-wing beliefs and politics were diametrically opposed to most of the political affiliations and goals of feminists and women's liberation ideologues, especially in light of the right wing's traditional suspicion of empowerment for women, its stance on abortion rights, and its low view of women in non-traditional roles.

The image Thatcher came to convey—an uncompromising believer in her own principles—was in line with her nickname, and was also captured by a line from one of her most famous speeches: "The lady's not for turning."[36] Though lauded by many, Thatcher's tough, conservative stance certainly did not fit the caring, empathetic feminine stereotype. To some, this combination of callous personality and harsh policy constituted a betrayal of her sex.

One of the high points of Thatcher's leadership was marked by Britain's successful pursuit of the war with Argentina over the Falkland Islands. Though many doubted both the campaign's wisdom and its possibility of success, Thatcher never wavered. As a result of the British victory, her popularity soared, both at home and abroad, and international opinion of the United Kingdom generally enjoyed an upswing.

Her political reign came to an end after many lost confidence in her leadership style, and she faced opposition within her own party when her approval ratings continued to decline. She insisted her approval ratings had nothing to do with her ability to win elections—after all, she did win three elections. She could no longer deny what was happening when the opposing party, which trailed for months, suddenly had a double-digit lead over Thatcher's Conservative party in the polls. Realizing that she would not have the votes to win another term, she resigned.

Love her or hate her, no one can deny Thatcher's place in politics and in world history. Whichever position one takes, it's clear that Thatcher advanced the cause of women in politics, creating a precedent for women to lead not only in the liberal spheres traditionally aligned with female concerns, but also to occupy the front ranks of the conservative forces. As with Sarah Palin, though I do not personally espouse Margaret Thatcher's politics, I have no choice but to salute her resolve and her refusal to be defined by society's opinion of what was "proper" or "expected" from a woman.

The Courage to be Different

All of the women profiled in this Chapter dared to envision possibilities for themselves that diverged from roles typically assigned to women by society or culture. They chose their own paths, and they traveled resolutely forward.

In doing this, they had to oppose the limiting stereotypes that hindered their progress. They had to transcend, to rise above the limitations placed on their dreams and ambitions by those who could not accept their "misbehavior."

In the next chapter, we'll meet three courageous women who, likewise, refused to allow themselves to be defined and delimited by others' expectations.

CHAPTER 3

Rise above Limitations

FOR CENTURIES, WOMEN OF ALL RACES HAVE BEEN FIGHTING TO BE TREATED WITH dignity and with respect, to be treated fairly and equitably whether they are mother, wife or employee. Many women's groups and activists have brought awareness to issues that affect women's rights, and the rights of women have been debated since the beginning of time. In 1848, the Women's Rights Movement began in upstate New York when a small group of women got together for tea and began to discuss their dissatisfaction with the limitations placed on women. They set out to form their own convention "to discuss the social, civil, and religious condition and rights of woman." Using the *Declaration of Independence* as a framework, The *Declaration of Sentiments* was drafted, detailing the unjust treatment of women.[1]

Very soon, the movement began to encounter fierce opposition from those—both male and female—who felt threatened by any notion that society's limitations on women's rights, roles, and aspirations were unjust and ought to be removed. When you think about it, such opposition is inevitable any time traditions or time-honored understandings are being threatened. For many, fear of the unknown prevents any consideration of new ideas on the basis of their own merits.

This is not only true for movements, but also for individuals.

When I began to question how things were being done at my organization, and especially when I began to take actions based on my convictions, opposition was not long in surfacing. In other words, as long as I was willing to go along to get along, I was seen as a team player and a valued colleague. When I began to think for myself and ask uncomfortable questions, I was labeled as trouble.

Once you begin your journey down the path you have chosen for yourself—if you are determined and persistent—you, too, will encounter those who will try to remind you of your "proper" place and, if necessary, to forcibly return you to it, by pointing out all the reasons why you can't do what you have set out to do. They will seek to enforce those limitations with methods that, while they may vary in degrees of harshness, are the same in their intent: to protect the very status quo to which they perceive you as a threat—to punish and halt your "misbehavior."

Sojourner Truth: "Ain't I a Woman?"

> *"If the first woman God ever made was strong enough to turn the world upside down all alone, these women together ought to be able to turn it back, and get it right side up again!"*

In her 1851 speech to the Ohio Women's Rights convention, an African American former slave and anti-slavery activist, Sojourner Truth, combined her anti-slavery message with an affirmation of the rights of all women in a famous speech, "Ain't I a Woman?" She discussed how men helped women over ditches and into carriages; however, this help was for white women, not black. Sojourner Truth posed to the convention the troubling question of why she was still treated as less than a woman.

Born a slave in about 1791 near Swartekill, New York, Sojourner Truth, or Isabella Baumfree, as she was then known, worked for several masters until she was sold to John Dumont in 1810. Some of her masters had been harsh or actually cruel. Dumont, though kindly disposed toward Isabella, made deceptive promises to her about setting her free.

Thinking about the deceptive promises made to Isabella by her master reminds me of my own experience at my former employer and of the misleading assurances made to me about my future with the organization. "If you fulfill certain obligations, we will make you a VP," they told me. After I fulfilled the obligations, they added more requirements, the list became longer and longer, and I soon realized that the promises were made in vain. We often put a lot of faith and trust in our leaders and superiors as Isabella did in her master; however, they are not always honest and at times they exploit vulnerabilities that we have as a result of our passionate beliefs. For Isabella, it was her freedom; for me it was not only the promotion but also my desire to prove that hard work and dedication often pay off. However, even if my own efforts were foiled by lies and ended in disappointment, I can look at myself in the mirror with my integrity intact.

Eventually, Isabella, after giving Dumont what she judged as a sufficient amount of labor to discharge her agreed-upon obligation, escaped to freedom a year before legal emancipation in New York, finding a safe harbor for herself and her infant daughter, Sophia, in the home of Isaac and Maria van Wagener. She would later say, "I did not run off, for I thought that wicked, but I walked off, believing that to be all right."[2] Most of us who have chosen to walk or run away from a terrible situation or circumstance come to understand the reasons for our decision, even if it takes us a while to get to that point. While walking away is painful for many reasons, we understand the bigger picture and believe that there are better and brighter days on the horizon.

Isabella later learned that a son she had borne while serving Dumont had been illegally sold to a slave owner in Alabama. With the assistance of the van Wageners, she took Dumont to court and prevailed, regaining custody of her son. She was the first black woman in America to sue a white man and win.

As I reflected on Isabella's fight for the son who was illegally sold into slavery and her taking her former master to court, it dawned on me that this was a pretty risky act that could have cost Isabella her life. However, she understood that a crime had been committed, knew the risks involved, realized the limitations placed on her as an emancipated slave, and made the decision to stand for what she believed was right.

She underwent a dramatic religious conversion and in 1843 changed her name to Sojourner Truth, stating that she had been summoned by the Spirit of God. She began traveling the country under the sponsorship of the Northampton, Massachusetts, Association of Education and Industry, an abolitionist organization, lecturing and preaching about the need for the abolition of slavery, women's rights, and religious tolerance. During this period, Truth met Frederick Douglass and other activists, spoke to the first National Women's Rights Convention, held in Worcester, Massachusetts, purchased a home in Northampton, Massachusetts, and had her memoirs published under the title *The Narrative of Sojourner Truth: A Northern Slave*.

Soon afterward, Truth spoke at the Ohio convention, delivering her famous speech, "Ain't I a Woman?" During the Civil War, she was active recruiting Union troops and in securing rights and relief for freed slaves. She spent a great deal of time in Washington, D.C., where she met President Lincoln and spearheaded efforts to desegregate the city's streetcars. Using tactics that would be echoed by later desegregation activists like Rosa Parks, Truth purposely rode on whites-only streetcars in order to bring the issue to public awareness and force action. Truth did not wait for a movement to effect change. Though she could have been content to wait for someone else to address the injustices, she decided that she could not idly stand by and do nothing.

After the Civil War, Truth continued her work for women's

rights and freedmen's relief, working unsuccessfully for seven years to convince the federal government to provide land grants for freed slaves. She also spoke out for penal reform and against capital punishment, and continued lobbying for women's rights until her death in 1883.

This woman, whose origins were from among the most disenfranchised of the disenfranchised, went on to provide counsel and advice to presidents, social leaders, and philanthropists. By refusing to accept the definitions and proscriptions forced on her by society, Sojourner Truth rose far above her humble beginnings to inspire millions—and continues to do so, even today. Perhaps most important, she recognized that even though she had personally achieved legal emancipation from slavery, she could not be truly free in the fullest sense until the unjust laws and conditions that allowed slavery and the subjugation of women to continue had been abolished and a fairer and more enlightened society had been secured. In other words, Truth believed that "equality for some" really meant "equality for none," and she was willing to risk her personal comfort, freedom, and reputation in order to oppose the evils of her day. Such courage and determination make her a fitting example for anyone who is determined to pursue a more fulfilling life, no matter the odds.

Betty Friedan: Defining the "F" Word

> *"The problem lay buried, unspoken, for many years in the minds of American women. It was a strange stirring, a sense of dissatisfaction, a yearning that women suffered in the middle of the twentieth century in the United States. Each suburban wife struggled with it alone. As she made the beds, shopped for groceries ... she was afraid to ask even of herself the silent question—'Is this all?'"*

Educator, author, lecturer, journalist, and activist Betty Friedan offers an example validating the axiom that no title or status is required for a person to make a difference or start a movement—only conviction. Graduating from Smith College in 1942, Friedan produced her groundbreaking work *The Feminine Mystique* in 1963, a title that is often credited with launching "Second Wave" feminism. She was also one of the founders of the National Organization for Women (and its first president), the National Women's Caucus, and the National Abortion Rights Action League.

Friedan was married and had three children with husband Carl Friedan. It was during her second pregnancy she recalls being fired for being pregnant.

> After I was fired for being pregnant, I was technically a housewife. And it was the era that I later analyzed, the "feminine mystique" era, [when] "career woman" was a dirty word. And so I didn't want a career anymore. [But] I had to do something. So I started freelancing for women's magazines.[3]

While Friedan enjoyed being a wife and mother, she was not satisfied with those being her only roles and sought other ways to satisfy her inner yearning to do and be more.

During a college reunion, she discovered that she was not the only woman who felt dissatisfied; several of her college classmates evidenced a similar discontentment. Friedan and her friends dubbed the phenomenon "the problem that has no name."[4]

Friedan noted that despite all the writing being done by and for women during the middle years of the twentieth century, no one was speaking about this unfulfilled yearning in the hearts of many women. Instead, women were being instructed and encouraged in how they might make their husbands and families happier and more successful; how they might make mealtimes more interesting; how they might cope with the myriad responsibilities of managing a household; how they might look, act, dress, and feel more feminine ... how, in short, they might learn to glory in their womanhood and pity the unhappy, discontented women who wanted to have professional, artistic, or other careers that did not in some way depend on their prowess as wives and mothers.

As she gathered more and more evidence of how widespread was the suffering and dissatisfaction of middle-class American women, Friedan devised an in-depth questionnaire and administered it to her classmates from Smith College to see how they were using the education they had received and what level of satisfaction they had with the lives they had chosen. The responses from the survey were troubling to Friedan. While she had expected the women to describe their lives as well adjusted and state that they were satisfied with the paths they chose, many of the mostly white, middle-class women who responded stated instead that they were not using their education and were dissatisfied with their roles; they felt their lives were not fulfilling.

This knowledge, in turn, forced Friedan to confront the limitations of her own role as a woman and whether she was using her education to its full potential. Friedan began developing the results of her research into articles that she submitted to some of the women's magazines for which she had been freelancing. But, she discovered:

> ...whatever I wrote was heretical. It offended the editors of the women's magazines. So after I had about four versions of it turned down, I said, "Hey, what's going on here?" Because I had never had an article turned down. And I realized that what I was saying was threatening, somehow, to the editors of these women's magazines. That it threatened the very world they were trying to paint, what I then called the "feminine mystique." And I would have to write it as a book, because I wasn't going to get it in a magazine. And the rest is history.[5]

Released in 1963, *The Feminine Mystique* became a bestseller. The book highlighted the results of the survey, documenting the dissatisfaction and loneliness these educated women felt in their roles as housewives and mothers. *The Feminine Mystique* was well received by many women who felt that there was more to life than being a wife and mother. It validated the deep-seated sentiments of many women who wanted more options than those American culture offered women at the time. For many women, Friedan's book was life changing and transforming. They felt less isolated, realizing that other women felt as they did. Still, *The Feminine Mystique* was quite controversial when it was published.

The response to the book was so overwhelming that Friedan realized "the problem that had no name" provided the impetus for a movement on behalf of women similar to what the N.A.A.C.P. had provided for African Americans during the fight for civil rights. Thus, "second wave" feminism, the spiritual daughter of the pioneering work done in the late nineteenth and early twentieth centuries by women like Elizabeth Cady Stanton, Sojourner Truth, and Susan B. Anthony, was born.

Throughout the remainder of the 1960s and 1970s Friedan and the National Organization for Women would seek to address gender equality and other rights for women. The movement challenged the status quo concerning limitation of the role of women to being wives and mothers.

As a result of the success of her book, she became the voice and the face of the second wave of feminism. As one of the founders and the first president of the National Organization for Women, she campaigned for issues such as gender equality for women, affordable childcare through federally funded childcare centers, full enforcement of Title VII of the 1964 Civil Rights Act to end sex discrimination, and promoting women in politics in order to effect and change policies that impact the rights of women. The movement Friedan helped bring into being had as its objective "to take action to bring women into full participation in the mainstream of

American society now, exercising all the privileges and responsibilities thereof in truly equal partnership with men."[6]

Friedan also founded the National Women's Political Caucus in 1971 and the National Association for the Repeal of Abortion Laws (NARAL) in 1969. She was responsible for publicly leading the Women's Strike for Equality that took place in 1970 in cities around the country. In New York, Ms. Friedan and tens of thousands of women of all ages marched down Fifth Avenue to publicize their campaign for equality, many carrying signs and banners that read, "Don't Cook Dinner — Starve a Rat Tonight!" and "Don't Iron While the Strike Is Hot." Some men joined the cause and marched with the women for equality. The event concluded with passionate speeches by Friedan, Gloria Steinem, Bella Abzug, and Kate Millett.

Years later, she advocated a feminist reclamation of the family and also sought to bring more men into the movement. She continued to push for change in laws governing childcare, parental leave, and flexible work schedules. Published when she was 71, Friedan's 1993 bestseller, *The Fountain of Age* criticized "the age mystique" and society's frequently patronizing treatment of the elderly. As passionately as she had advocated for women two and three decades before, she now urged society to embrace new, positive roles for older citizens.

Inevitably for anyone—male or female—as focused and ambitious in her goals as Friedan, she had a number of critics. She was often faulted for her direct, abrasive approach when addressing issues and further criticized for creating or tolerating division among women. Some felt that especially in its early days the movement was more concerned with the rights of middle-class, married white women and ignored minorities, the poor, and other marginalized groups, notably lesbians. Some of her eulogists, including other influential feminist writers such as Germaine Greer, said, even while paying tribute to her life and influence, that in her life

Friedan was often imperious, demanding, and outraged when she failed to receive the deference she believed she deserved.

In spite of the criticisms, no one can deny her influence as well as her work championing the rights of women, for which she received accolades, awards and honorary degrees. Perhaps she will always be known as the suburban housewife who started a revolution by writing *The Feminine Mystique*. It is certainly true that rarely has a single book been responsible for such sweeping, tumultuous, and continuing social transformation. By refusing to bow to those who would have kept her safely categorized as wife, mother, homemaker, and nothing else, Betty Friedan shifted the landscape of American law and society.

Shirley Chisholm: Pioneer for Inclusion

> *"One distressing thing is the way men react to women who assert their equality: their ultimate weapon is to call them unfeminine. They think she is anti-male; they even whisper that she's probably a lesbian."*

Years before Hillary Clinton, Sarah Palin, or even Geraldine Ferraro saw their names listed as candidates on the tickets of national parties, Shirley Chisholm became the first black woman to run for President of the United States. A politician, educator, and author, Chisholm was also the first black woman in Congress, elected in 1968 to represent New York's 12th District, a role in which she served from 1969 to 1983.

Born Shirley St. Hill on November 30, 1924, in Brooklyn, she moved to Barbados at the tender age of three and was raised by her grandparents until the age of 10. Her working-class parents remained in New York during the Depression in order to earn money to help provide for their children.

Shirley was noted for her intelligence early in life and recognized the value of an education at a young age. She did well in school and took to heart the advice imparted to her by her grandmother about the value of education and the importance it would have in her future. She attended Brooklyn College where she graduated *cum laude* with an education degree; she also received a master's degree in early childhood education in 1952 from Columbia University. She wanted to be a teacher to make a difference in society by helping children. Her first job was at a childcare center in Harlem, where she worked for several years.

After serving as director of a day care center, she served as an educational consultant with the Division of Day Care in New York. While attending college, one of her white male professors realized her potential, noting her strong speaking and rhetorical skills. Under his encouragement, Chisholm joined the debate team and rose to captain. The professor encouraged her to pursue a career in politics.

It is important to recognize the people who have shaped our lives in a positive manner. This professor helped to shape Shirley's political future because he saw her potential and did not try to limit her aspirations because of her race or her gender. Instead, he encouraged her to join the debate team and even to pursue a career in politics.

I recently visited the national headquarters of the NAACP, the nation's oldest civil rights organization, in Baltimore. I felt a sense of pride when I looked at the historical timelines and pictures that graced the walls. One image in particular caught my eye: the historic "March on Washington" held on August 28, 1963. I was gratified as I looked at the various signs carried by the marchers. However, I was deeply moved when I saw how many white people were holding hands in solidarity with African Americans marching and shouting for freedom. On that historic day, freedom knew no color and no gender.

As I reflected on Shirley's white male professor encouraging her to pursue politics, I was reminded that Americans across gender and color lines fought for freedom, and we should not forget this fact when we try to paint a particular group as racist or a particular gender as sexist or inadequate.

I believe in diversity. I am the woman I am today because of the knowledge, lessons, and insights I've gained from people of different backgrounds: the many people who saw my potential and nothing else. What a boring world it would be if we all looked and thought alike! Accepting people for who they are shaped Shirley's legacy and was displayed when showing compassion for one of her opponents later in her career.

In 1964, Chisholm was elected to represent her district in the New York State Legislature. Then 40 years of age, she was the first black woman ever to be elected to public office in Brooklyn. While in office, she wrote and submitted several bills, four of which were signed into law. The most significant bill was the extension of unemployment insurance coverage to domestic workers. Four years later, she became the first black woman elected to the United States Congress after defeating Republican opponent James Farmer for the right to represent New York's 12th Congressional District.

Chisholm did not go to Congress with the objective of fitting in, but rather to represent her constituents and to be their voice in Congress. As a freshman in Congress, she refused the assignment that was given to her: the House Agriculture subcommittee on forestry and rural villages, believing that this committee would have little to do with issues affecting her district. Instead, she felt her experience and background in education made her an ideal candidate for the education committee. Despite her objections, however, she was assigned to serve on the veteran's affairs committee. While this was not the assignment Chisholm felt she was best prepared for, she did feel that she would at least be able to fairly represent veterans from her district. She fought hard for the rights of veterans and also led efforts to help veterans become more educated about the rights to which they were entitled. As a freshman legislator, she also became one of the founding members of the Congressional Black Caucus.

In 1972, Chisholm became a household name when she made a bid, along with eight white males, for the Democratic nomination to the presidency. Walter Cronkite introduced Chisholm's candidacy to America on the *CBS Nightly News* by saying, "A hat, rather, a bonnet has been tossed into the presidential ring today: that of Congresswoman Shirley Chisholm."

In the speech announcing her candidacy, she declared,

> I stand before you today as a candidate for the Democratic nomination for the Presidency of the United States of America. I am not the candidate of black America, although I am black and proud. I am not the candidate of the women's movement of this country, although I am a woman, and I am equally proud of that. I stand here now without endorsements from many big name politicians or celebrities or any other kind of prop. I do not intend to offer to you the tired and glib clichés which for too long have been an accepted part of our political life. I am the candidate of the people of America. And my presence before you now symbolizes a new era in American political history.[7]

Later, Chisholm would say,

> I ran for the Presidency, despite hopeless odds, to demonstrate the sheer will and refusal to accept the status quo. The next time a woman runs, or a black, or a Jew or anyone from a group that the country is "not ready" to elect to its highest office, I believe that he or she will be taken seriously from the start.... I ran because somebody had to do it first.[8]

Many, who felt that she had no chance of winning because she was a black woman, resented Chisholm's candidacy because of the perception that she would take votes from candidates who had a chance of winning. Even some feminists who agreed with her platform preferred to back a candidate whom they believed could win; many of these supported Sen. George McGovern as the Democratic candidate. Feminists have been criticized for being divisive and not supporting the advancement of feminism even when presented with the opportunity to do so. After campaigning in twelve states, Chisholm won 152 delegates to the Democratic convention after candidate Hubert Humphrey, in a symbolic gesture, released his black delegates to Chisholm. Nevertheless, McGovern would win the nomination.

In response to Democratic candidates' failure to invite Chisholm to participate in a televised debate, Chisholm filed a complaint with the Federal Communications Commission to break the lock on televised debates during the presidential campaign. She successfully filed a motion with the federal court that subsequently enabled her to talk directly to a national television audience. She was determined to make the most of this opportunity to attract voter attention to her platform on education, employment, health care, and the rights of minorities, women, and gays.

Chisholm created controversy when she visited rival George Wallace in the hospital soon after his shooting during the 1972 presidential campaign. Though many questioned why she would darken the door of an avowed and vocal segregationist, this act was a simple reflection of Chisholm's caring nature—even toward those who opposed what she stood for. Significantly, several years later as Chisholm was working for passage of a bill to give domestic workers the right to a minimum wage, Wallace got her the votes of enough Southern congressmen to push the legislation through the House—one of her proudest legislative achievements. Later, she would say of her visit to Wallace's hospital room, "I believe there is good in everybody; maybe that's a weakness I have."[9]

In her 1970 autobiography *Unbought and Unbossed* she wrote,

"In a just and free society, it would be foolish that I am a national figure. Because I was the first person in 192 years to be at once a congressman, black, and a woman proves, I think, that our society is not yet either just or free."[10] Throughout her career, Chisholm stood on her convictions and refused to be defined by party politics or racial affinities.

Her decision to cross party lines and endorse the confirmation of Republican Nelson A. Rockefeller as Vice President from the floor of the House in 1974 drew scrutiny and criticism. Years later in an interview with a *Washington Post* reporter, she responded to criticism about her support of Rockefeller and her hospital visit to Wallace. "I don't take one incident of a person's total life and hang the person with it forever."[11] Rockefeller was supportive of Chisholm when she was in the state legislature. This willingness to do what she thought was right, rather than what was politically expedient, often put her at odds with many of her supporters. She once said, "My greatest political asset, which professional politicians fear, is my mouth, out of which come all kinds of things one shouldn't always discuss for reasons of political expediency."[12]

After retiring from Congress in 1982, she taught at Mount Holyoke College in South Hadley, Massachusetts. She also helped found the National Political Congress of Black Women in 1984. Shirley Chisholm died at her home in Daytona Beach, Florida, on January 1, 2005.

During her career, Chisholm faced opposition, not only from white males, but also from women and other black politicians. Still, she steadfastly refused to accept limitations on her aspirations, her efforts, or her capabilities. Not only that, but she was deeply conscious of both her example and her responsibilities to those who would come after her. In living her life as she did and forging ahead against all opposition, Shirley Chisholm left a legacy and blazed a trail for anyone who dares to dream beyond the circumstances of birth, race, or gender.

According to Chisholm,

> Many women have given their lives to political organizations, laboring anonymously in the background while men of far less ability managed and mismanaged the public trust. These women hung back because they knew the men would not give them a chance. They knew their place and stayed in it. The amount of talent that has been lost to our country that way is appalling. I think one of my major uses is as an example to the women of our country, to show them that if a woman has ability, stamina, organizational skill, and a knowledge of the issues, she can win public office. And if I can do it, how much more hope should that give to white women, who have only one handicap?[13]

Clearly, the three women profiled in this Chapter faced significant opposition in their lives because of the paths they chose. By refusing to be limited by society's assumptions about them—whether due to their race, their gender, or both—they placed themselves squarely at odds with the majority, and that almost always spells trouble. The true pioneers, however, are those who persist, even in the face of resistance, strengthened in their resolve by their firm conviction that what they are doing is what must be done.

In the next chapter, we will learn the stories of four women who refused to back down when faced by opponents—even, in one case, by those who would take her life.

CHAPTER 4

Persist against Opposition

A FRIEND ONCE TOLD ME ABOUT A MISSIONARY HE KNEW WHO WORKED FAITHFULLY for many years in a part of the world where a deeply entrenched state religion made his work very difficult—even dangerous, sometimes. Yet he never tired of carrying out what he believed was his calling from God, no matter how difficult things got, how lonely he felt sometimes, or how far away success often seemed to be.

Once, when the missionary was asked how he felt about facing such constant opposition, he said, "Dogs only bark at things that move." In other words, he knew if the work he was doing was not important, he would not face any opposition or difficulties. As long as he was steadily going about the business of following his divine mandate, it was inevitable that he would face complaints, threats, difficulties, and trials—sometimes, trials in a real courtroom. This story reminds me of what Paul said in one of his letters: "… a great door for effective work has opened to me, and there are many who oppose me" (1 Corinthians 16:9). For Paul, the opportunity to do something great was accompanied by strong opposition.

It seems like facing opposition for doing good is inevitable. As Sarah Palin said, it doesn't take much effort to go with the flow—even a dead fish can do it. But when we seek important, life-changing accomplishments, we almost always find ourselves swimming against the current. The same principle holds true in the human body: If you want a muscle to get stronger and larger, you must force it to face resistance. If you want a muscle to weaken and atrophy, all you have to do is make sure it never has to do anything.

When I resolved to make a real difference at my former employer, I began to face opposition—ultimately costing me my job. In the beginning, I wondered what I had done wrong, but the experiences of the women in this Chapter helped me to understand that the opposition I faced was for doing the right thing.

Joan of Arc: Spiritual Icon of a Nation

> *"One life is all we have and we live it as we believe in living it. But to sacrifice what you are and to live without belief, that is a fate more terrible than dying."*

Joan of Arc was a French peasant girl born on January 6th around the year 1412 in the village of Domrémy. At the time of her birth, France and England were at war and a truce was in place; however, not all of France's enemies were external; factions within the French royal family meant the country was divided—in many ways, at war with itself.

From the tender age of twelve, Joan began to have visions that she described as saints and angels whom she could see and touch. The city of Orléans had become the primary focus of the English, and the saints in Joan's visions urged her to drive out the English and Burgundians. "I was thirteen when I had a Voice from God for my help and guidance. The first time that I heard this Voice, I was very much frightened; it was midday, in the summer, in my father's garden."[1] She reportedly told her parents about the visions and voices and they responded by telling her that her visions were merely dreams. She was able to convince her parents that the visions and voices were real and her mission was to drive out the English from her beloved France.

There are those who felt that Joan's visions were due to extreme stress brought on by the effects the 100-year war with England was having on France, its small villages, and especially Joan's parents. Many doubted that God would give Joan, a mere child, an important mission or appear to her in this manner.

In the Bible, God speaks directly to prophets, servants, and others. He even used angels to accomplish his mission. For example, in the Old Testament book of First Samuel, God spoke directly to Samuel and also had a vision and a plan for Samuel, who was younger than Joan at the time of God's call.

Joan eventually convinced the French leadership, including Charles VII—the Dauphin, heir to the French throne—of the authenticity of her mission from God and that she could serve her nation, lead troops, lift the siege of Orléans, and retake other English-held territories. Charles initially had doubts; however, Joan was able to convince him and his counselors by making some remarkable predictions of military successes that came to pass for the French.

Although Charles was convinced, he had some theologians examine her to see if she was genuine and also to satisfy himself that she was not a witch or a heretic, either of which would be seen as nullifying the spiritual legitimacy of any victory she might help him achieve. Joan convinced her examiners of both her sincerity and her innocence, and subsequently a seventeen-year-old peasant girl was given control over an army and allowed to lead them into battle.

Within a year Joan had led the French army to victories at Orléans, Patay, and Troyes. She also liberated other towns from English control and in mid-July made a triumphal entry into Reims for the coronation of King Charles VII. After Charles became king, he and Joan disagreed on the future of the war; Charles favored a temporary truce while Joan urged an immediate offensive to liberate Paris. Charles prevailed, however, and the pause in hostilities worked to the advantage of the Duke of Burgundy, who used the time to fortify Paris against the advancing armies led by Joan of Arc.

She was captured in a relatively minor skirmish near Compiègne just less than a year later. Though it was customary at the time for royalty and important military captives to be ransomed, Joan's family was poor and had no financial resources to make the attempt. Many historians have condemned Charles VII for failing to procure Joan's release; indeed, it does seem remarkable that after all this young woman had done to revive the flagging hopes of a nation under attack, she would simply be allowed to remain in the hands of her captors.

Not that Joan didn't make attempts to save herself. On one occasion, she jumped seventy feet from a tower in Vermandois where she was being held, her fall broken by the soft ground of a dry moat. However, she was recaptured and transferred to a different prison.

As I studied the story of Joan of Arc, I perceived certain parallels with my own career as well as the stories of many of my female colleagues from different backgrounds and organizations: women who worked under extreme conditions, undertook projects where particular initiatives were implemented and, in many instances, revitalized their respective organizations. Often these initiatives resulted in contracts or clients that breathed new financial life into the organizations, saving jobs and careers. Many of these women worked long hours, put their health and well-being on the line, and in some instances, neglected their personal relationships to support their bosses and the organizations that they believed in.

You may be like these women. Perhaps you helped your boss transition into a new role and, after his feet were firmly planted, he forgot your help. Perhaps you later learned that you were disposable, a mere steppingstone. The old adage, "What have you done for me lately?" rings true, all too often. There are so many women who work behind the scenes to ensure that our bosses and our organizations are successful; however, many times we fail to get the recognition we deserve. We may even come to be seen as a threat or a thorn in the boss's side.

I remember a conversation with the CEO from my former

organization who told me that I was becoming too powerful in my role; he and others were uncomfortable, and he said that I needed to remember that my role was merely one of support. I was taken aback by his comments. After all, I was in charge of a department that provided support to the entire organization. I perceived myself as a strategic partner and worked hard to perform the responsibilities of my position. Nonetheless, like Joan, I was eventually abandoned by those I had supported and assisted to turn the organization around.

Joan of Arc was eventually turned over to pro-English authorities. They decided that the best way to de-legitimize Charles VII and his coronation was to accuse Joan of witchcraft or, at the least, of religious heresy. Inevitably then, her mockery of a trial had nothing to do with her leadership style or what she accomplished on the battlefield, but rather about religion and political maneuvering.

Even though no real evidence could be found against her and she was denied her right to legal representation under canon law, Joan was found guilty and condemned to death by burning at the stake. Her accusers tried to force her to recant the authenticity of the voices and visions that had convinced her to place her faith in God and to lead French soldiers in battle against the English. When she refused, she was condemned for heresy and sorcery and was burned at the stake.

Pope Callixtus III convened a retrial some years later and, with the aid of clerics from all over Europe, reviewed the testimony and other trial proceedings. Joan's conviction was reversed, and the pope declared her to have been an innocent martyr. She was canonized a saint in 1920 and remains one of the patron saints of France.

All through history, women have been successful in leading roles. They have fought hard and put their lives on the line for the principles and people that they believe in. Women can be great leaders without having to be ruthless, conniving, or deceptive. I think poor leadership qualities can be found in both genders; however, excluding someone from leadership because of an unfounded gender stereotype is inappropriate. While it is true that there have been women like Cleopatra and Jezebel who used their power and gender for manipulative purposes, it also cannot be denied that there have been men like Stalin and Hitler who have wielded power brutally and with disastrous results for their own people. It is also without question that women as leaders have altered the course of history. Joan of Arc will always be remembered for staying true to her calling—she stood by her convictions and led her people to freedom. She believed in truth, integrity and loyalty—in the end, she paid the ultimate price.

Anucha Browne Sanders: Sexual Harassment and the Hostile Work Environment

> *"It is the responsibility of workplace leaders to set the standard for a comfortable working environment."*

In 2007, former NCAA standout and New York Knicks executive Anucha Browne Sanders won a multimillion-dollar sexual harassment lawsuit against New York Knicks coach and general manager Isiah Thomas and Madison Square Garden, the owner of the New York Knicks. The settlement was hailed as the largest sexual harassment award on record.

Her lawsuit against Thomas and Madison Square Garden was in response to being fired for complaining about sexual harassment and a hostile work environment that she endured at the hands of Thomas that began with his hiring by the Knicks in 2003.

According to details from the lawsuit, Thomas created a hostile work environment for Browne Sanders by making unwanted sexual advances towards her, calling her derogatory names, and professing to be in love with her. "He referred to me as a bitch repeatedly and [called me] 'ho' in private conversations, and many of his sentences started with the word 'bitch.'"[2]

By all accounts, Browne Sanders followed the protocol in place at her organization for dealing with harassment. Before the issue escalated, she addressed her concerns with Thomas and Knicks management; however, she felt her complaints were not taken seriously or addressed in a satisfactory manner, as the harassment continued. She accused management, in fact, of fostering the harassment. According to Browne Sanders,

> Management did little to nothing. There was one meeting that we had to try to resolve any type of confusion in terms of roles and responsibilities, and I was told to accommodate him, that this was his working style, and I was told things like, "Oh, that's just the way Isiah is." The breaking point for me was when I had been complaining for a year and a half. When I realized what was happening to the women around me, I said "This is ridiculous." That was the breaking point.[3]

Thomas allegedly asked a Knicks cheerleader to flirt with referees before a game against the Nets, and the cheerleader "reluctantly" did as she was asked. Browne Sanders stated, "Isiah asked her to go into the referees' locker room and make them happy. I asked her to tell me what that meant and she said, 'Well, he wanted me to flirt with the referees.'"[4]

Browne Sanders did not set out to be a hero or to be the defender of women's rights, great or small. She simply wanted to be successful in her role and to work in an environment that was free from sexual and other forms of harassment. After realizing that other women were being subjected to the types of harassment she faced, she decided to do something about it.

In another incident in 2005, a member of Browne Sanders' staff told her that she had consensual sex with New York Knicks point guard, Stephon Marbury. The woman, who was an intern, admitted the sex was consensual and reportedly told Browne Sanders that "she did not believe she could say 'no' because of who Marbury is."[5]

Realizing that the organization fostered an environment of sexual and other forms of harassment, Browne Sanders began addressing the issues with management. After many of her complaints were not addressed, she challenged management on how the complaints and inappropriate behavior were being handled. After numerous complaints, she was eventually fired for "poor performance." Shocked but not surprised, she realized that her firing was retaliatory and sued the organization as well as Isiah Thomas for sexual harassment. "I made the decision to sue because when I finally pressed [the issue of] sexual harassment and hostile work environment with management, they fired me." [6]

According to *New York Daily News* sportswriter Michael O'Keefe, "During the trial, Browne Sanders described Thomas as a foul-mouthed bully who was unable to work with smart and successful women. [Madison Square] Garden President Steve Mills came across as an ostrich who would rather bury his head in the sand than deal with sexual harassment complaints."[7]

Madison Square Garden's management portrayed Browne Sanders as a poor performer who was fired for "an inability to fulfill professional responsibilities."[8] Her firing was seen to many as retaliation because Browne Sanders had been consistently promoted over the course of her career with the organization. She received salary increases and bonuses as well as several glowing performance evaluations based on her performance.

My personal experience, as well as that of colleagues and friends, indicates that many organizations respond inappropriately to complaints of sexual and other forms of harassment by retaliating, creating a hostile work environment, or using alleged poor performance as a reason to terminate or discipline someone they view as a thorn in their sides. At the same time, there are high-quality organizations that invest in training and development to create harmonious working environments.

From a human resources perspective, it is important for employees who believe they are experiencing harassment of any type to document dates, conversations, and events and to keep records and copies of performance evaluations, emails, and any other documentation that can validate their complaints and establish timelines for future inquiry. This will often help employees in the event they are faced with retaliation or a hostile work environment as a result of challenging the status quo or addressing inappropriate behavior.

Browne Sanders kept records and details of conversations, performance evaluations, records of bonuses and promotions granted, and other related information. She created a paper trail through proper documentation of her experience with the New York Knicks, even though she initially had no intent of going to trial. Nevertheless, as a result of her termination and the subsequent lawsuit she filed, her documentation became extremely valuable in helping her to make her case. The trial lasted about three weeks and in the end a jury made up of both women and men found Madison Square Garden, the owner of the New York Knicks, and Isiah Thomas liable for sexual harassment. As a result, Madison Square Garden had to pay $6 million for fostering a hostile work environment and $2.6 million for its retaliatory firing of Browne Sanders. In addition, Madison Square Garden's chairman, James Dolan, was fined $3 million; however, compensatory damages were not awarded against Thomas. Browne Sanders was pleased with the verdict although she was not pleased with the circumstances that led to the verdict,

> What I did here, I did for every working woman in America, and that includes everyone who gets up and goes to work in the morning, everyone working in a corporate environment. It is my hope that all

> women will be able to work in an environment that is free of discrimination and harassment and that any woman who stands up for her rights will be taken seriously by her employer rather than retaliated against.[9]

She also encouraged women in similar situations to speak up: "The only way you make change is by being there; being silent never makes change, so speak up."[10] Speaking up for what is right is not necessary just in cases of sexual and other forms of harassment—we should speak up when we are exposed to or witness injustices against any person or group.

During and after the trial, the issues of race and loyalty surfaced, as both Browne Sanders and Thomas are African American. Many people in the African American community feel that dirty laundry within the African American community should not be aired in a public forum. Not surprisingly, many of these same misgivings were aired when Anita Hill, an African American woman, came forward with allegations of sexual harassment against Clarence Thomas, an African American man.

When asked about this issue during an interview, Browne Sanders responded, "African American women are just supposed to keep quiet about this kind of thing; [they are told] that they should not speak publicly against a successful African American man, and that this is just not good for the community to have this kind of dirty laundry, if you will, aired publicly."[11]

However, prior to the trial, Browne Sanders followed proper protocol by privately addressing her concerns with Thomas as well as management. She also raised the race issue to Thomas when trying to discuss their work relationship and the significance of their race in the positions that they held:

> I did have a discussion while I was at work with Isiah about the importance of us trying to figure out a …

> professional environment or relationship. Because, you know, where else in sports would you see an African American president of the team, an African American president of Madison Square Garden and an African American woman who was a senior vice president of the franchise? So I did bridge that with him. But in the end, this was not about keeping quiet. This was about raising an issue that affects so many women across corporate America and saying, "You know what? This is just simply unacceptable, regardless of your color, regardless of who you are, where you are."[12]

While it is important to speak up when you are exposed to sexual or other forms of harassment, as with any decision that has career and personal implications, you should always consider the cost. Many women and even men who come forward to blow the whistle or take a stand against inappropriate behavior worry about their futures and their families, precisely because of the type of treatment Browne Sanders received from her employer. These individuals worry about being blacklisted and being unable to find employment in the future. They lose relationships with colleagues with whom they have worked for years; after all, many of their colleagues want to protect their own careers and fear associating with a whistle blower or an employee who stands up against the organization to address inappropriate behavior or challenge the status quo. Others who choose not to come forward may simply look for employment elsewhere rather than endure the mental anguish of character assassination, an investigation, or a trial. They fear putting their personal and professional lives on display.

Coming forward or taking a stand is a difficult and painful decision and not to be taken lightly. Indeed, the implications of this decision often involve not only the employee's present circumstances and potential future stress and embarrassment but also the future direction of an organization and the way it treats employees. Usually, when a company refuses to address inappropriate behavior and an employee leaves without formally addressing the cause for the complaint, current and future employees can expect the behavior to continue and to be subjected to a hostile work environment. Browne Sanders says it best: "Being silent never makes change."[13]

Browne Sanders's predicament also highlights another deep chasm in the corporate workplace: the scarcity of women in executive positions. Harassment and sexism are a few of the barriers women face when trying to climb the corporate ladder, and many minority women will argue that they face racism as well. Though we live in twenty-first–century corporate America, women still have to constantly prove themselves by working three to four times harder than many of their male counterparts; at the same time they must battle negative stereotypes about their race and gender and, in some instances, face harassment.

In the last century, the demographics of the workplace have changed dramatically, as more minorities and women enter the workforce. This phenomenon poses additional challenges for employers. It is encouraging that employers have been implementing programs and other initiatives to help deal with the changing demographics of the workplace. Indeed, many of these programs go beyond affirmative action and other rights under Title VII of the Civil Rights Act. Some organizations cite the business case for diversity and inclusion which, studies show, can positively impact an organization's bottom line and give it a competitive advantage in the global marketplace.

Organizations that fail to take proactive steps to protect and foster respect for all employees, regardless of race, gender, or ethnicity, may find themselves, more and more, defending themselves from the rightful complaints of people like Anucha Browne Sanders: employees who, rather than making a valuable and strategic contribution to the ongoing success of the organization, are resorting to the legal system to force the organization to recognize their basic human rights.

Gloria Steinem: "A woman without a man is like a fish without a bicycle"

> *"I've learned only one thing: No matter how hard it is to do it, it's harder not to do it. Then you're stuck with wondering ..."*

Gloria Marie Steinem was born on March 25, 1934, in Toledo, Ohio. She became an activist to fight against the systems, laws, and societal assumptions that subjugate and oppress women. She helped shape the debate and raised awareness of women's disenfranchisement. Because of her fight for equal opportunity for women and the breaking down of gender roles, Steinem has been hailed as one of the most important feminists of the twentieth and twenty-first centuries.

Self-described as a radical feminist, Steinem is also a bestselling author and journalist. As the cofounder of *Ms. Magazine*, Steinem has won various awards for her contributions to society and her advancement of women's issues. She is widely regarded, along with Betty Friedan, as one of the founders of the second wave of feminism in America.

Her grandmother Pauline Steinem was a suffragette, and many believe that Gloria was born to be a feminist: that feminism was in her blood and was also brought to the fore by her family's background.

She had a difficult childhood, as she traveled around the country with her parents in a trailer that served both as a residence and her father's place of business as an antiques dealer. Her parents divorced when she was about ten years old, perhaps partially as a result of her mother's mental illness. According to Steinem, her mother's illness, along with the caregiving responsibilities she provided for her mother, helped opened her own eyes to some of the social injustices facing women. In spite of the difficulties and challenges she faced as a child, she completed high school and graduated with honors from Smith College. After graduating, she spent a few years in India, including two years on a Chester Bowles Asian Fellowship, an experience that opened her eyes to issues such as hunger and poverty outside the United States. Her first book, *A Thousand Indias*, was a guidebook for the Indian government. She also began writing freelance articles for newspapers.

After returning to the United States, Steinem had various freelance jobs for magazines and newspapers and continued to pursue her writing career. In the 1960s she worked for a political satire television program, *That Was the Week That Was.* In 1963 she published the article "I Was a Playboy Bunny," getting a job as indicated in the title, then detailing her work experience and the poor treatment of women in the Manhattan Playboy Club. After the Playboy bunny article, offers to write and other assignments evaporated. She reportedly regretted writing the article because it impacted her finding work and other assignments.

In 1971, Steinem along with Betty Friedan, Bella Abzug, and Shirley Chisholm, founded the National Women's Political Caucus. The mission of the caucus was to identify and encourage women to run for political office. In 1972, she co-founded and served as editor of *Ms. Magazine, a magazine for and about women* that addressed feminist issues including reproductive rights, employment discrimination, sexuality, and gender equality. The magazine was extremely well received by women as it was among the first publications of Second Wave Feminism to provide a platform and forum that addressed issues important to women. Steinem also cofounded the Ms. Foundation for Women, a nonprofit organization that pioneered the concept of giving money to programs that addressed the specific concerns of women.

During the 1972 presidential election, she campaigned for George McGovern and financially contributed to his 1972 campaign for the presidency; however, she later withdrew her support when she felt disrespected by McGovern's campaign staff, believing that McGovern "still [didn't] understand the women's movement."[14] She was further disappointed when he removed the issue of abortion from the party's platform. Critics like Germaine Greer felt that Steinem had the opportunity to call McGovern on his hypocrisy regarding his platform on abortion and did not do enough to expose him. This issue added to some of the other criticisms Steinem received later on about cherry-picking which candidates and/or issues she chose to support or criticize. Nevertheless, throughout her life, she fought for and actively participated in many grass roots organizations that supported the advancement of women.

In the 1980s and 1990s, she found herself fighting for health issues of her own as she was diagnosed with breast cancer in 1986 and trigeminal neuralgia in 1994. Although her health issues were challenging, they never deterred her from fighting for the many rights of women and other marginalized groups. In the 1990s, she cofounded Choice USA, a nonprofit organization that mobilizes and provides ongoing support for reproductive choice to younger women. She publicly supported Anita Hill during the controversy surrounding Hill's testimony in connection with Clarence Thomas's confirmation hearings.

In addition to fighting for the rights of women, she has also fought for and brought awareness to the prevention of child abuse, co-producing a documentary on the topic for HBO. She is also a bestselling author—some of her books include *Revolution from Within: A Book of Self-Esteem; Outrageous Acts and Everyday Rebellions; Moving Beyond Words; and Marilyn: Norma Jean.*

While Steinem has been acclaimed for leadership in protecting and advocating for the rights of women, including laws and court cases such as Title IX and Roe v. Wade, she and the women's movement generally have also been criticized for being out of touch with twenty-first–century women as well as for politicizing women's issues and not being supportive of women who do not share her political views. As a result, "feminist" has been categorized as a dirty word, based on public perception of how issues are handled within the movement. Steinem and NOW have been criticized for having a win-at-all-costs attitude, an issue that was raised during the Shannon Faulkner case amid allegations that the organizations overlooked Faulkner's health and failed to consider the emotional toll the fight was having on her.

During the Clinton impeachment hearing, when asked if President Clinton should be impeached for lying under oath, she responded by saying, "Clinton should be censured for lying under oath about Lewinsky in the Paula Jones deposition, perhaps also for stupidity in answering at all." She felt the affair was "no one's business" as there was "no coercion, harassment, or violence."[15]

Many felt that she did not go after Clinton or support Lewinsky the same way she supported Anita Hill during the Clarence Thomas hearing, and alleged it was because Clinton was a Democrat and Thomas was a Republican. However, Steinem saw it differently, "When Monica testified, she was very clear that she wanted and initiated this relationship."[16] According to Steinem, Hill was subjected to a hostile work environment as Thomas regularly and graphically described sexual practices and pornography—the type of hostile work environment that sexual harassment laws were intended to reduce.

Apparently, her view of female empowerment even extends to a woman's right to initiate and approve of a sexual encounter with a male superior—including the President of the United States, in the case of Monica Lewinsky. In a 1998 *New York Times* op-ed, Steinem's support of Clinton confused many because it seemed somewhat contradictory. One the one hand, Steinem agreed that Mr. Clinton's behavior was inappropriate; however, critics of the op-ed say that it sent the message that it doesn't matter how inappropriate your behavior is as long as you support or help advance women's issues. Clearly, all women did not agree with her opinion and it further divided the movement; many believed Steinem and other feminists not only failed to understand the views of all women, but they also did not and should not speak for all women. There are some who believe that the divisiveness and lack of unity that exist among women are often created when issues of class, race, and politics are involved and may be the reasons the movement has not evolved as the force it promised or aspired to be.

I believe it is irresponsible to blame any single person or an entire movement for the lack of unity that exists among women. Women have come a long way but there is a still a lot of work to be done. We cannot let petty distractions or divisions deter us from our goal. Steinem has brought attention to many key issues facing women: abortion rights, lack of access to affordable and high-quality child care, the lack of social supports for poor women and their children, nonexistent or inadequate health care, the continuing wage gap, and others.

She was an active participant in the 2008 presidential election; early on, she endorsed Hillary Clinton. Once again, she took a lot of heat for an op-ed in the *New York Times* that many found divisive. She stated that gender discrimination was an even bigger issue than race and defended her views by saying that black men were given the vote a half a century before any women were.

Steinem was seen as pitting gender against race with her speculation that women are more oppressed because of their gender:

> Gender is probably the most restricting force in American life, whether the question is who must be in the kitchen or who could be in the White House. This country is way down the list of countries electing women and, according to one study, it polarizes gender roles more than the average democracy.[17]

There are many who feel that "there is some truth in Steinem's comparison, albeit only by considering isolated incidents." Many black women feel that some black men are more readily accepted in the 'old boys' network' by virtue of being male, they have access to systems and organizations that are not accessible to women. On the other side of the coin, there are many black men who would argue that they still cannot get a taxi cab because of their race and gender and are still racially profiled while driving.

Whichever side of the argument one may be on, Gloria Steinem's implication regenerated the old race vs. gender debate about which group has it worst. "By casting the debate between black men and white women (Barack vs. Hillary), Steinem, some have suggested, renders the woman of color invisible, reaffirms the binary black-white paradigm of race, and demands we take a side in the epic battle between race and gender."[18] This argument only deepens the divide, "a divide keenly felt by women of color who have long felt alienated by feminists like Steinem." In many ways, "these women felt that being asked to choose between Obama and Clinton was the same as being asked to choose whether race or gender were their most important attributes."[19] The fact is, most of us wouldn't be able to choose between our gender and our racial or ethnic heritage; both are vital parts of who we are! And, in a just society, we would never be asked to.

> If we're really ready to take equal pride in breaking all the barriers, then how can we be expected to make the call between voting for any candidate based on racial or gender identity? Regardless of whom we decide on, by making the identity politics of our candidate a factor in our decision, we are implicitly establishing a "separate and unequal" relationship between race and gender barriers that only fuels the continued clash between race activists and feminists.[20]

Race and gender are all-encompassing issues that still permeate our society. To her credit, Steinem also said on this topic,

> I'm not advocating a competition for who has it toughest. The caste systems of sex and race are interdependent and can only be uprooted together. The abolition and suffrage movements progressed when united and were damaged by division; we should remember that.[21]

In September 2008, Steinem wrote an op-ed titled, "Wrong Woman, Wrong Message," in which she critiqued Sarah Palin's candidacy for vice president. Like many feminists, Steinem felt that Sarah Palin benefited from the work of the women's movement; however, she believed Palin's political philosophy did more harm than good. While she praised the accomplishments and powerful presence of women in American politics, she feared what would happen if the wrong woman were chosen for the job.

> Here's the good news: Women have become so politically powerful that even the anti-feminist right wing are trying to appease the gender gap with a first-ever female vice president. But here is even better news: It won't work. This isn't the first time a boss has picked an unqualified woman just because she agrees with him and opposes everything most other women want and need. Feminism has never been about getting a job for one woman. It's about making life more fair for women everywhere. It's not about a piece of the existing pie; there are too many of us for that. It's about baking a new pie.[22]

Steinem continues to advocate for the advancement of women's issues in a male-dominated world; however, she refuses to let anyone—male or female— dismantle the work that so many have fought to enact and protect. She continues to challenge the status quo despite her critics—many of whom are women. Some of her views are liberal and some are radical. She encourages choices for women and supports those who do the same.

From Steinem, I have also learned that over time your views on a particular issue can change as systems and structures change. This belief is evidenced by her marriage at age 66 to South African businessman David Bale, a move that surprised many people, especially feminists, in light of her 1970s rallying call, "A woman without a man is like a fish without a bicycle." She was married to Bale for only three years before he died of cancer. She responded to her critics by saying that marriage had evolved and now allowed women much more freedom.

Beginning with her difficult childhood, much of which was spent as a caretaker for a mentally ill mother, continuing to her writing and journalism careers amid the growing upheavals of the civil rights and women's rights movements, and extending to the rough-and-tumble of presidential politics, Gloria Steinem has continued to speak up for women. She has also continued to speak her mind on the issues, even when her views have been poorly received by those who might be expected to be her allies. She is unquestionably one of the most important leaders of second wave feminism, and remains, at this writing, as determined and outspoken as ever.

Lilly Ledbetter: Equal Pay for Equal Work

> *"It was very humiliating to learn that I was being paid so much less than my white, male peers for doing the exact same job and doing it well."*

Prior to the Senate Judiciary hearings in September 2008, few people knew of Lilly Ledbetter and her fight against Goodyear Tire and Rubber Company for sex discrimination relating to equal pay.

Her case reached the Supreme Court after a series of charges, rulings, and appeals.

Ledbetter became a household name during the 2008 presidential campaign when several members in Congress introduced the Lilly Ledbetter Fair Pay Act. In January 2009, the United States Congress passed the Lilly Ledbetter Fair Pay Act, which President Barack Obama signed into law. Prior to 2008, Ms. Ledbetter spent about ten years fighting to receive equal pay for equal work.

In 1979 Lilly went to work at the Goodyear Tire & Rubber plant in Gadsden, Alabama, as a line manager and was later promoted to area manager. Over the course of her career, she received training and development to help her effectively perform her duties. Working in a male-dominated industry and plant presented many challenges for Ledbetter, as many of the men she worked with or supervised did not like a woman telling them what to do. "They'd say, 'I take bossing from a woman at home—I'm not doing it here,'"[23] she reported.

However, she eventually earned the respect of her colleagues and subordinates through her hard work as well as her dedication to the organization. Proving her gender was not a handicap, she worked as hard as her male colleagues, working long hours and extra shifts, and when needed, she filled in on the production line despite being a manager. "When people saw, especially men, that I worked and carried my weight, their attitudes changed,"[24] she said. It is important to note that many people prefer to work with colleagues and subordinates who can effectively perform their jobs; however, many women and minorities do not always get a chance to prove themselves because they are often excluded from positions and organizations as a result of discrimination.

Ledbetter was accepted by most of her colleagues and subordinates; however, she realized that not all of her colleagues and supervisors treated her with respect; some supervisors did not give her the information she needed to effectively perform her job. She found a way around this dismissive behavior by forming relationships with other managers who shared needed information with her.

During her time at Goodyear, Ledbetter was subjected to discrimination as well as sexual and other forms of harassment. She filed a sexual harassment claim with the Equal Employment Opportunity Commission (EEOC) when a supervisor asked her for sexual favors in return for a good performance evaluation. As a result of her complaint, the supervisor was reassigned; however, Ledbetter says she became known as a troublemaker around the plant and someone to be avoided. She did not pursue a lawsuit for sexual harassment because she really did not want to take her employer to court. By coming forward, she opened herself up to more harassment.

In most organizations, pay increases are based on compensable factors—such as the market rate for the position, responsibilities associated with the job, cost of living, and budget—and other factors such as performance. The amount of the increase (merit or cost-of-living adjustment) is determined by how well you performed during the previous year and whether or not you achieved goals and objectives that were established during your performance planning and review process. At Goodyear, salary increases were based on performance and supervisor ranking; the better your performance review the higher your merit increase, while a poor or average performance review equaled a lower increase. At Goodyear, Ledbetter's performance reviews were at the low end of the scale and as a result, she received small merit increases.

In addition, salary and wages often determine employees' basic life insurance as well as pension benefits. For Ledbetter, this meant her pension and other benefits were affected by her low salary increases, as her retirement benefits were based on her average preretirement earnings. The many years of inequity resulted in a substantial amount of money in lost wages and benefits.

In July 1998, someone left an anonymous note in her mailbox showing her salary as well as the salaries of three of her male colleagues who had the same job titles and performed the same responsibilities. She was being paid $3,737 a month while her male colleagues were compensated in the range of $4,286 to $5,236 a month.

Ledbetter was unaware of what her colleagues made until she received the note, as Goodyear's personnel policies forbade employees from discussing salaries.

> Someone slipped me an anonymous note showing my name with three males ... doing the exact same job and the base pay, and mine was drastically different than theirs. And I really—when I saw that, it took my breath away. I felt humiliated. I felt degraded.[25]

This policy is not unique to Goodyear; conflicts arise among employees when discussing wages and salaries. It's easy to understand this, given the very personal nature of income. Furthermore, employees generally do not understand all the various components that factor into pricing a job. Some organizations do publish wages; however, many of the positions are union or government positions based mainly on job and tenure and not necessarily education, experience, and performance. Even though Ledbetter experienced sexual harassment during her career at Goodyear, she did not believe she would face pay discrimination from Goodyear; she believed Goodyear was a reputable organization. After all, they had several government contracts—surely they followed the law, she believed.

It is unclear as to whether or not she addressed the issue through internal channels; however, she was off work the day after receiving the anonymous note and subsequently filed a complaint with the EEOC.

After filing her complaint in July 1998, Ledbetter felt her supervisors were being retaliatory when they reassigned her to a job that required her to lift heavy Hummer tires for inspection.

Subsequently Goodyear announced the closure of the Gadsden, Alabama, plant and decided to cut a number of jobs. Ledbetter believed that she was being "forced into early retirement" and accepted a buyout package that was offered to her.

In November 1998 Ledbetter filed a lawsuit with the District Court against Goodyear, claiming pay discrimination under Title VII of the Civil Rights Act of 1964 and the Equal Pay Act of 1963. On the Equal Pay Act claim, the District Court found in favor of Goodyear because under the Act, pay differences that are based on merit increases are allowed and not necessarily discriminatory.

The court, however, allowed the Title VII and other claims to proceed to trial. Ledbetter claimed that her performance evaluations were unfair because of her gender and as a result, she had received significantly lower raises and increases than her male colleagues. Goodyear claimed that their evaluations were non-discriminatory and focused only on worker competence, even though Ledbetter received a Top Performance Award in 1996. The court ruled in Ledbetter's favor and awarded her back pay and punitive damages of more than $3.3 million, though this was reduced to $300,000, the statutory cap.When asked what she thought about the verdict, Ledbetter said that she was happy with the ruling; however, she knew that Goodyear would appeal. As she predicted, Goodyear appealed the district court's ruling to the Eleventh Circuit Court of Appeals, arguing that all claims to damages before September 1997 were void as a result of the statute of limitations for filing discrimination claims under Title VII of the Civil Rights Act.

The Eleventh Circuit Court of Appeals reversed the district court's decision, ruling that Ledbetter could sue only for allegations regarding pay discrimination that occurred less than 180 days before her initiation of the EEOC process in March 1998.

Disappointed with the appellate Court's ruling, Ledbetter filed a writ for judicial review with the U.S. Supreme Court. The Supreme Court granted the writ and heard the appeal. In a 5–4 ruling, the Supreme Court upheld the ruling of the Eleventh Circuit Court of Appeals. The Court ruled that employees like Lilly Ledbetter who are subject to pay discrimination must file a claim within 180 days of the employer's original decision to pay them less—even if the employee continued to receive reduced paychecks and even if the employee did not discover the discriminatory reduction in pay until much later.

In her dissent, Justice Ginsburg read the following from the bench:

> The Court's insistence on immediate contest overlooks common characteristics of pay discrimination. Pay disparities often occur, as they did in Ledbetter's case, in small increments; cause to suspect that discrimination is at work develops only over time. Comparative pay information, moreover, is often hidden from the employee's view. Employers may keep under wraps the pay differentials maintained among supervisors, no less the reasons for those differentials. Small initial discrepancies may not be seen as meet for a federal case, particularly when the employee, trying to succeed in a nontraditional environment, is averse to making waves.
>
> Pay disparities are thus significantly different from adverse actions "such as termination, failure to promote... or refusal to hire," all involving fully communicated discrete acts, "easy to identify" as discriminatory.[26]

Justice Ginsburg in her dissent invited Congress to correct the Court's misinterpretation of Title VII: "[t]he ball is in Congress' court ... the Legislature may act to correct this Court's parsimonious reading of Title VII."[27]

On January 22, 2009, the United States Congress enacted The Lilly Ledbetter Fair Pay Act of 2009, and it was signed into law by President Barack Obama on January 29, 2009. The bill amended the 180-day statute of limitations for filing an equal-pay lawsuit under the Civil Rights Act of 1964. After signing the Lilly Ledbetter Fair Pay Act into law, President Obama made the following statement:

> It is fitting that with the very first bill I sign—the Lilly Ledbetter Fair Pay Restoration Act—we are upholding one of this nation's first principles: that we are all created equal. Lilly Ledbetter didn't set out to be a trailblazer or a household name. She was just a good hard worker who did her job—and did it well—for nearly two decades before discovering that for years, she was paid less than her male colleagues for the very same work. Over the course of her career, she lost more than $200,000 in salary, and even more in pension and Social Security benefits, losses she still feels today.
>
> Now, Lilly could have accepted her lot and moved on. But instead, she decided that there was a principle at stake, something worth fighting for. While this bill bears her name, Lilly knows this story isn't just about her. It's the story of women across this country still earning just 78 cents for every dollar men earn—women of color even less. I know that if we stay focused and keep standing for what's right, we will close that pay gap and ensure that our daughters have the same rights, the same chances, and the same freedom to pursue their dreams as our sons.[28]

Lilly Ledbetter considered the cost before deciding to address sexual harassment and pay discrimination against Goodyear. Nevertheless, she was subjected to retaliation and found herself working in a hostile work environment. She felt that her equal pay lawsuit was for all women who faced pay and other forms of discrimination.

As a result of her courage, a law bearing her name was passed. She may have lost the battle, but she won the war for all those who face pay discrimination. Ledbetter lives on a nominal retirement income from Goodyear that she characterizes as "paycheck to paycheck." She says, "I'm just thrilled that this has finally passed and sends a message to the Supreme Court: You got it wrong."[29]

By persisting in the face of opposition and refusing to quit, the women profiled in this Chapter made important headway toward addressing historical injustice and inherently unfair treatment of women, both in the workplace and at home. Though opposed, maligned, harassed, and threatened, they persisted in doing what they believed was right.

In the next chapter, we will meet more women who refused to remain silent in the face of wrongdoing and injustice, even though they knew their actions would subject them to hostility, if not actual physical danger. Their stories can inspire us all toward greater courage and conviction to do what is right, no matter the personal cost.

CHAPTER 5

Speak Up for Justice

My experience working in Human Resources has provided me with the wonderful opportunity to meet people from various backgrounds and walks of life. While leading a department such as HR is not for the faint of heart, I would be remiss if I did recognize the significant impact of the many lives I've come in contact with—many that have changed me as an individual—both personally and professionally. HR professionals will tell you, our departments are typically not the place where people in most organizations will voluntarily spend a lot of time. While HR professionals wear many hats, it is a profession and a function that is not always viewed in a positive light for various reasons. In some organizations, the HR department is generally viewed as a means to an end at best, and your last stop on your way out the door at worst. After applying for the position at the organization, HR is the one department that you'd want to hear from to find out if you got the job, how much you'll be making, and your start date.

HR is where you sit and daydream during your new employee orientation, wishing you were doing your job instead of finding out about company procedures; it is where you find out that no, the company's insurance plan will not cover the cost of the hot tub in your backyard without significantly more documentation than "I've got back trouble"; it is the department you'd go to if you were having problems with a co-worker or a supervisor; it is the place you find out that your service with the organization is no longer needed and more than likely the place where you'll receive your pink slip, or, where you'd go, pink slip in hand, to find out how long you have before your severance package runs out—and it's never long enough. HR professionals, though absolutely necessary for the efficient and lawful functioning of most large enterprises, are usually valued primarily for whatever benefits they can provide at the moment. Otherwise, we mostly tend to be tolerated ... and that's in a well-run organization.

The organization where I last worked was not a well-run organization, as I found out to my chagrin only after I had accepted the position. In all fairness, I must admit that I ignored several red flags during the interview process, perhaps because I believed so strongly in the mission of the organization. However, I took the job, and before long, I realized that my predecessors left behind a mess that desperately needed to be cleaned up. I vowed to myself to go about the business of fixing what was broken and making the organization stronger, more compliant with regulations and best practices, and a place where employees would be proud to work.

In the process, I began ruffling the feathers of many who were satisfied with the status quo. I must admit that I never understood this opposition, as the organization was in desperate need of change. So many policies and processes had been neglected for a very long time.

Change and transformation are always uncomfortable for those who don't understand the need for change and the benefits it can bring. Often, these individuals continue to mistrust agents of change even when the case for change is communicated effectively. There is an old adage: "Even good soldiers get wounded in battle." While I understand that being attacked is part of the job and comes with the territory, it would have been a lot easier if I had received support from my superiors. Unfortunately, when change became uncomfortable, it was easier to blame HR than to explain that change was necessary in order for the organization to survive.

During the difficult times, I seriously questioned why I was working sixty or more hours per week while getting almost no support for my efforts. The long hours, opposition, and lack of support had become significant by the time I came in contact with Ms. Vivian, a member of the housekeeping staff.

Ms. Vivian was responsible for cleaning my office as well as all the offices in my department and most of the offices on the second floor. Her job performance was far from stellar. As a matter of fact, Ms. Vivian was a mediocre employee at best—most of the staff, including her colleagues, had a fairly low opinion of her, and her relationship with her supervisor was broken beyond repair. Despite all that, for reasons I could not have explained at the time—even to myself—I decided to get to know Ms. Vivian.

When I first met her, it was as if I had known her for a long time; we connected in a way I could not explain. I felt compassion for her and the type of work she did. I have always been fascinated with people, their lives, and their chosen paths. I am always curious about their childhood, their relationships with their family, their children, and their community.

As she cleaned my office (barely), she would tell me about her family, her children, and her coworkers. I found out Ms. Vivian was someone's mother, grandmother, sister, daughter, and friend; she was a human being—a child of God. She was indeed special.

Too often we miss out on great relationships and getting to know people because we look at their status and what they do and judge them without even getting to know them. We should all remember Jesus' charge to take care of "the least of these."

I soon figured out that much of the harsh, disagreeable exterior that Ms. Vivian showed the rest of the world was due to the simple fact that Ms. Vivian was not in the best of health—in other words, she felt lousy, most of the time. She had chronic obstructive pulmonary disease (COPD), so just catching a breath was a struggle for her. This meant that oxygen wasn't getting to her brain in the proper amounts, affecting her mood—and not for the better. It also didn't help that she was a smoker. In addition, her job involved cleaning offices, requiring her to dust or use cleaning chemicals as part of her daily routine.

From one perspective, Ms. Vivian should have been fired a long time ago. But from my perspective, she was a person who needed my help. She could not perform the essential functions of the job because of her health. Nevertheless, her supervisors wanted her gone every time she was not able to perform the job. It's not that she did not want to do her job; she couldn't, even when she tried. There were some who felt I was protecting someone who was dead weight; however, I decided to put my knowledge of employment law to work on Ms. Vivian's behalf. After all, part of HR's role is to help people.

Ms. Vivian was eligible for leave under the Family and Medical Leave Act based on her illness. However, Ms. Vivian was stubborn and did not always take the necessary steps to ensure that she received the protection she was entitled to under the law. For example, she was given paperwork numerous times and never took the time to complete it.

I found out that she did not have a clear understanding of what she needed to do, so I went over all the paperwork in detail. When I saw she was still struggling, I personally worked with her doctors to make sure she got the paperwork completed in a timely manner. She was granted an initial leave that provided her with job and benefits protection; however, this protection was only for twelve weeks.

After her twelve-week leave was exhausted, I advised her that she could apply for a personal leave of absence to extend her leave for another thirty days. This infuriated some of her managers, who knew she could not return to work after the twelve weeks and were looking forward to her termination. However, I believed Ms. Vivian was entitled to all of the benefits that were available to other employees.

At the end of the thirty days, she was not able to come back to work, so I helped her apply for Social Security. She had to be disabled for five months to qualify for disability payments from Social Security. However, she was about a month away from being able to receive regular Social Security payments, so it worked out.

I remember times when she did not have gas to get to work or to go back and forth to the doctors; I would give her gas money. I never asked her to repay me, but Ms. Vivian was a very proud woman and did not want to take what she considered handouts from anyone—including me. So, in return, she baked me some of the best pound cakes I have ever tasted.

Ms. Vivian talked fondly of her sons and her grandchildren—one son lived in North Carolina and Ms. Vivian always expressed her desire to spend more time with him and her grandkids; the last year of her life she had the opportunity to do so. On July 12, 2010, Ms. Vivian died. I was honored to be able to speak at her funeral, sharing some of the experiences I had with her. My mission was made clear to me when I heard the Holy Spirit say, "Mission accomplished." This was a huge confirmation and affirmation for me, as my goal was still to make a positive difference in the organization where I worked, even though at times I questioned why I was there. However, I was able to make a positive difference in the life of Ms. Vivian—by being compassionate.

It is true that Ms. Vivian was not an exemplary employee. It may even be true that she should have been fired. But this was a poor woman whose negative attitude toward the world was due in large part to the way people treated her—people who had no idea what she was struggling with. She tried fighting for herself but the fight was too big for her. Ms. Vivian actually taught me a lot: about not taking myself too seriously, and about being true to my calling.

All through my career at that organization I was an advocate for those without a voice. I was able to help people that my organization felt were not worth helping. And looking back, I realize that I was, in my own way, trying to redress the injustices that are inherent in a system that is often blind to the limits and difficulties that ordinary people must deal with. Each of us, it seems to me, has a responsibility to do what we can to make the world a fairer, more just place. By helping Ms. Vivian, I suppose I was trying to change one small corner of the world.

In this chapter, you will meet other women who have refused to remain silent and passive in the face of injustice. They were willing to take on a fight they didn't start, although not all of them were able to see it through to the end. As you read their stories, let their courage enter your mind and find its way to the center of your heart.

Rosa Parks: Taking a Stand by Taking a Seat

> *"People always say that I didn't give up my seat because I was tired, but that isn't true. I was not tired physically, or no more tired than I usually was at the end of a working day. I was not old, although some people have an image of me as being old then. I was forty-two. No, the only tired I was, was tired of giving in."*

Dubbed the "Mother of the Modern-day Civil Rights Movement," Rosa Parks was a seamstress who became a civil rights activist because of her refusal to give up her seat on a bus to a white man. As a result, she was arrested for refusing to obey the orders of the bus driver.

According to Parks, "When he saw me still sitting, he asked if I was going to stand up, and I said, 'No, I'm not.' And he said, 'Well, if you don't stand up, I'm going to have to call the police and have you arrested.' I said, 'You may do that.'"[1]

In 1955, Montgomery, Alabama, had a city ordinance that segregated passengers by race. Conductors and drivers were given the power to assign seats to accomplish that purpose; however, no passengers would be required to move or give up their seat and stand if the bus was crowded and no other seats were available.

Over time and by custom, however, Montgomery bus drivers had adopted the practice of requiring black riders to move whenever there were no white-only seats available. But on this day, Rosa Parks had decided that enough was enough.

While the officer was taking her away during her arrest, she asked, "Why do you push us around?" The officer responded, "I don't know, but the law's the law, and you're under arrest." She later said, "I only knew that, as I was being arrested, that it was the very last time that I would ever ride in humiliation of this kind."[2]

At the time of her arrest, she was a member of the National Association for the Advancement of Colored People (NAACP) and served as the secretary to the president of the Montgomery chapter. Many leaders of the black community got together to discuss how they would respond to Parks' arrest as well as air their frustrations about the effects of segregation. Soon, they announced plans for a boycott of the Montgomery bus system.

Meanwhile, Parks was tried and found guilty of disorderly conduct and violating a local ordinance. Parks appealed her conviction and formally challenged the legality of racial segregation. Years later, reflecting on her actions, Parks said,

> I did not want to be mistreated, I did not want to be deprived of a seat that I had paid for. It was just time ... there was opportunity for me to take a stand to express the way I felt about being treated in that manner. I had not planned to get arrested. I had plenty to do without having to end up in jail. But when I had to face that decision, I didn't hesitate to do so because I felt that we had endured that too long. The more we gave in, the more we complied with that kind of treatment, the more oppressive it became.[3]

The Montgomery bus boycott would become one of the largest and most successful actions against racial segregation in history. The day of Parks' trial, volunteers distributed leaflets requesting riders not to ride the bus.

> We are ... asking every Negro to stay off the buses Monday in protest of the arrest and trial. You can afford to stay out of school for one day. If you work, take a cab, or walk. But please, children and grown-ups, don't ride the bus at all on Monday. Please stay off the buses Monday.[4]

The day of the boycott, black commuters carpooled or rode in cabs that were black-owned; riders were charged the same fare as the bus. Others walked as far as twenty miles to protest Parks' arrest and the segregationist laws that precipitated it.

Prior to the boycott, no one could have predicted its outcome or the impact it would have had on Montgomery. The action lasted for over a year; many of Montgomery's public buses were idle for months, severely impacting the public transit company's finances. Eventually, the law requiring segregation on public buses was lifted due to the financial impact of the boycott and the negative attention it brought to Montgomery.

Many people who take a stand against injustice are not motivated by a desire for fame or a place in history. Instead, most come forward because they are tired of unfair treatment or policies and laws that discriminate against individuals or groups. Rosa Parks sparked a movement because she was tired of segregation and what it did to blacks in her city. However, there were consequences to her decision, even beyond the humiliation of her arrest and trial. She was fired from her job as a result of her actions and was the target of segregationist threats. Nevertheless, her "civil disobedience"—what many considered "misbehaving"—helped to lift segregation on Montgomery buses; it also propelled Martin Luther King Jr. to the forefront of the civil rights movement.

None of us should downplay the accomplishments of the Montgomery Bus Boycott or the struggles of the civil rights movement. People were beaten and killed in the struggle to gain many of the rights we enjoy today. Although Title VII of the Civil Rights Act was eventually enacted years after the boycott, many are still marginalized and suffer injustice.

As British statesman Edmund Burke said more than two centuries ago, "All that is required for evil to triumph is for good men to do nothing." Rosa Parks reached the point where doing nothing was no longer an option. As in her case, there are times in each of our lives when we need to take a stand and say, "Enough is enough."

Susan B. Anthony: Pioneer for Women's Rights

> *"Cautious, careful people, always casting about to preserve their reputation and social standing, never can bring about a reform. Those who are really in earnest must be willing to be anything or nothing in the world's estimation, and publicly and privately, in season and out, avow their sympathy with despised and persecuted ideas and their advocates, and bear the consequences."*

Susan Brownell Anthony was born on February 15, 1820, in Adams, Massachusetts. She was exposed to reform movements and liberal ideas from an early age; her family supported the anti-slavery movement as well as the temperance movement. As a teenager, she collected petitions opposing slavery, even though collecting such petitions was prohibited at the time.

The beginning of the fight for women's suffrage can be traced to the drafting of the Declaration of Sentiments, presented at the first women's rights convention in Seneca Falls, New York, in 1848. The idea for the convention was born during Elizabeth

Cady Stanton and Lucretia Mott's visit to the World Anti-Slavery meeting in London. Both Stanton and Mott were looking forward to speaking at the convention but were denied the opportunity to speak from the floor or to be seated as delegates because of their gender. They realized that while they were fighting for the rights of slaves, women were not treated as equal and had few rights. They both decided that a national convention was needed to bring awareness to and support for securing equal rights for women.

In 1852, at the Woman's Rights Convention in Syracuse, New York, Susan B. Anthony joined the cause, arguing that "the right women needed above every other ... was the right of suffrage."[5] Anthony spoke and campaigned tirelessly to change the way women and other marginalized groups were treated. She spent most of her life petitioning for the rights of women, including the right to receive an education equal to that available to males.

Early in her life, she had a fear of public speaking based partly on self-consciousness about her appearance. She would overcome this fear; for most of her adult life, she delivered between 75 and 100 speeches and lectures per year as she crusaded tirelessly to achieve the vote for women and to speak out for equality in matters of divorce and property ownership.

Her mother Lucy, also a progressive thinker, participated in movements supporting women's rights. She attended the Women's Rights Convention in Seneca Falls, New York, in 1848 and signed the Declaration of Sentiments along with her husband and daughter.

In 1839, Anthony left home to become a teacher and to help support her family, which had suffered financially in a recent financial panic. Her first teaching job was at a seminary. Next, she taught at the Canajoharie Academy, rising to the position of headmistress of the Female Department. Noticing that women teachers sometimes earned a mere fourth of their male counterparts' salaries despite sharing identical duties, Anthony became a fierce advocate of equal pay for women.

After moving to Rochester, New York, she became involved

in the temperance movement, which was strongly allied with the women's movement because of the widespread belief that alcohol abuse often led to domestic violence against women. She did not get involved in the movement until 1851, however, as the roles of women were limited within the temperance movement. This further convinced her that women must win the right to speak in public and to vote. As a result, Anthony formed the Daughters of Temperance. Her work within the temperance movement provided her with the opportunity of meeting Elizabeth Cady Stanton and together they brought further awareness to, and continued the fight for, women's suffrage.

Anthony's observations of hypocrisy among various churches led her to distance herself from organized religion, a decision that caused a backlash from adherents of various religious groups.

In 1869 Anthony, with Elizabeth Cady Stanton, co-founded the National Women's Suffrage Association. Though Stanton would later fault Anthony for her narrow focus on the single issue of the vote rather than a broader spectrum of women's rights concerns, the two were the leading forces in the women's rights movement for most of the latter half of the nineteenth century.

Anthony helped develop a code for seamstresses in New York that required equal wages. She also campaigned for women to participate in public discussions, a right that was at that time afforded only to men. In 1870, Anthony was happy with the passing of the Fifteenth Amendment; however, it only gave black men the right to vote and she was very disappointed that women were not included. She was arrested in 1872 for illegally voting in the presidential election. Though she maintained that the Fourteenth Amendment to the Constitution gave all Americans the right to vote, she was convicted and sentenced to pay a fine. However, she stated in court that she would not pay it—and she never did. She continued to work vigorously for women's right to vote by petitioning Congress and the state legislatures as well as publishing her own newspaper. Susan B. Anthony's tireless efforts helped pave the way for the passage of the Nineteenth Amendment in 1920—fourteen years after her death.

There is an old adage that says, "It's not the size of the dog in the fight but the size of the fight in the dog." Many brave men and women fought for many of the rights we now enjoy, including the right to vote. In a democracy, we can positively effect change by using our vote to impact decisions on the issues that are important to us. Indeed, it is often said, "if you don't vote, you don't count." Had it not been for the work of pioneering activists like Susan B. Anthony, women's voices would not be heard and would not count. No wonder she and her peers made the exercise of this most fundamental right of a free society the most important goal of their untiring efforts.

On July 2, 1979, the U. S. Mint released the Susan B. Anthony coin in Rochester, New York, the home of Susan B. Anthony. She was the first woman—other than symbolic figures like Lady Liberty—to be honored by having her likeness appear on a circulating United States coin. It was a fitting tribute to her persistence, vision, and unyielding commitment to justice for all.

Anita Hill: The Courage to Face Criticism

> *"Testifying has helped me understand that one individual's behavior and actions make a difference. That my actions are important to people other than myself."*

Prior to the Browne Sanders trial in 2007, Anita Hill had already given new meaning to the term sexual harassment during the Senate confirmation hearings of Supreme Court Justice nominee Clarence Thomas in the early 1990s.

Hill's testimony regarding harassment she endured while working for Clarence Thomas heightened awareness of sexual harassment and helped pave the way for women like Anucha

Browne Sanders to stand up against sexual and other forms of harassment.

With the retirement of Supreme Court Justice Thurgood Marshall in 1991, President Bush nominated Clarence Thomas, an African American judge, to replace Justice Marshall. Some viewed Thomas as a token because of his race, while others, because of Thomas's conservative bent, felt his nomination was part of Bush's political agenda.

Indeed, many felt Thomas's views were too conservative on the issues that were important to them, such as abortion and affirmative action. Some civil rights organizations felt that Thomas's presence on the Supreme Court would undo much of what Justice Marshall fought hard to accomplish. Others felt he lacked the required experience because he had served only a few years as a federal judge. Into this swirling political debate came Anita Hill.

At the time of the hearings, Hill, an African American woman, was a law professor at the University of Oklahoma. During the hearings, Hill testified that Thomas used his position at both the Department of Education and the Equal Employment Opportunity Commission (EEOC) to pressure her for dates, and that he also made sexually explicit comments "about acts he had seen and pornographic films involving such matters as women having sex with animals, women having group sex, and rape scenes."[6] Hill also testified that Thomas commented about her body and whether her hair or her dress made her more or less sexually attractive to him. When she protested and voiced concerns about his comments and behavior, Hill alleged that Thomas ignored her concerns.

Thomas denied the allegations and later said that the hearings were "a high-tech lynching for uppity blacks."[7]

Hill was criticized for waiting eight years after the alleged harassment to come forward with her allegations, raising suspicions as to her motives. Some people thought she was being used as a ploy by many of the organizations that opposed Thomas's nomination and his conservative views. Her decision to wait eight long years before coming forward made a lot of women nervous about supporting her publicly.

Hill cited many reasons for waiting eight years, including not being able to get the vivid pictures of Thomas's sexual comments out of her head. She also discussed how her decision was impacted by the prospect of having Thomas, as one of the nation's supreme jurists, render decisions on legal issues that could affect millions of women. In her book *Speaking Truth to Power* she explains how she came to the attention of the Senate Committee overseeing the confirmation of Clarence Thomas as Supreme Court Justice; she was sought out because several Washington insiders knew of her experiences while working for Thomas. Hill denied that her testimony was a political ploy.

In my experience, there are many women who do not come forward to complain about sexual and other forms of harassment. In most cases, sexual harassment is at the hands of someone with power, such as a boss. This is not surprising, since sexual harassment is usually about control. Many victims of sexual harassment have to make a difficult choice when deciding whether or not to come forward. On the one hand, they fear what coming forward might do to their reputation, their livelihoods and their careers. On the other hand, if they do not come forward, they become victimized, as the harassment may continue and there are no guarantees it will stop. They also have to bear the stress and burden of working in an uncomfortable situation, which ultimately affects job performance.

If you are ever put in a situation where you are being harassed or are uncomfortable because of the discussions going on in your presence, you must say something, even if it's only, "I am uncomfortable with this discussion," or "I am not sure that this conversation is appropriate." By doing this, you have taken the first step towards addressing the inappropriate and harassing behavior. You never know where the abuser may end up or how he or she may shape policies that will affect the lives of others. It is also important to share your experience with someone you can trust if you are not comfortable going to a boss or superior. You should also document dates, discussions, times, and other information concerning the behavior that is creating your discomfort.

Although Hill waited to go public with her allegations, she did discuss her experience with others, a fact that was later verified. There were other employees interviewed who were either witnesses to or experienced Thomas's behavior.

As a result of the intense media scrutiny of the hearings, Hill became a household name. She was hailed as a heroine by many women for coming forward to answer intimate and embarrassing questions about her work environment as well as her personal life—at a time when it was not popular to do so. She considered the cost before deciding to put her own reputation on the line to bear witness to behavior that was inappropriate and that still affected her emotionally after eight years.

Thomas's eventual confirmation to the Supreme Court was upsetting to those who opposed his nomination, especially women who felt that the Senate did not take Hill's allegations seriously enough. At the time of the confirmation, the Senate was dominated by men and voted 52–48 to confirm Thomas as an associate justice of the Supreme Court. After the hearings, more women became involved in politics; a record number won seats in the Senate and the House in 1992. Some political pundits attributed the record number of seats won by women in the Senate and the House to the Thomas confirmation hearings and the awareness the hearings brought to women's issues.

The Hill-Thomas controversy had other long-term consequences beyond its impact on Thomas's nomination to the Supreme Court. Awareness of sexual harassment in the workplace heightened considerably. According to Equal Employment Opportunity Commission filings, sexual harassment cases increased following the hearings, and awards to victims suing under federal laws nearly quadrupled.

When asked about the hearings, Hill stated,

> If you think about the way the hearings were structured, the hearings were really about Thomas's race and my gender. What people can't really understand is that women can come forward on their own. What I wanted was for everyone listening to understand that these things mattered—not necessarily for me, but in this particular forum they mattered in terms of whether or not we were getting a person who should sit on the Supreme Court.[8]

Many wondered what happened to Hill after the public hearings; most assumed she quickly returned to leading a normal life. Instead, she continued battling public perceptions as well as health issues that were exacerbated by the hearings. Congress passed a resolution to investigate the leak of an FBI interview with Hill about Thomas. In Oklahoma, politicians called for her to resign her academic post. She also cited a lack of support from the black community. As would happen years later in the matter between Anucha Browne Sanders and another black man named Thomas, these critics felt that the hearings should not be used as a public forum to air dirty laundry between African Americans.

At the University of Oklahoma Law Center, a research endowment in Hill's name was challenged and obstructed by the state legislature, despite receiving sufficient donations from supporters. She became a lightning rod; many who publicly supported her during the hearings were hounded by anonymous calls and letters and chose to withdraw their support rather than endure the abuse. Hill eventually resigned from the University of Oklahoma as a result of the intense scrutiny and political pressure placed upon the university.

As I have said before, both history and my personal experience indicate that anyone who considers taking a stand for an issue should consider the cost. For publicly testifying about her experiences with Clarence Thomas, Anita Hill paid a hefty price with her health, her career, public scrutiny, and humiliation. Clearly understanding the potential personal costs, she said,

> I don't know that you can do something and not jeopardize your career—even today. I tell people to understand what their support is. Can you count on somebody within your institution to support you and support your right to go forward? ... [I] ndividuals should understand the policies and procedures and think about the potential results of an unwanted outcome.[9]

Many believe that the Senate did not understand or failed to acknowledge questions of power, control, and what it is to be in a hostile work environment. Troubling to many was the fact that Thomas was in charge of the very agency responsible for enforcing federal laws against racial and gender discrimination. However, the hearings soon focused not on whether Thomas was qualified or fit to serve on the Supreme Court, but rather on Hill's character and motives. Examples of this shift in focus include Sen. Alan Simpson's whispered aside—captured by a microphone—that Hill's testimony was "sexual harassment crap." She was asked by Sen. Howell Heflin, "Are you a scorned woman? Do you have a martyr complex? Do you have a militant attitude relative to the area of civil rights?"[10]

Hill commented,

> Although Simpson apologized after the hearings ... he could not take back the twin messages [his comment] sent: that sexual harassment is not real, and that complaints about sexual harassment should be met with "real harassment." I will not count the

> number of times ... that I have been threatened with sodomy, rape, assault, and other forms of sexual and nonsexual violence. Some of the callers have used almost the same words: "Now you will know what real harassment is like."[11]

In their 1994 book *Strange Justice: The Selling of Clarence Thomas*, Jane Mayer and Jill Abramson published the results of their interviews with former female employees of Thomas, some of whom said he had demanded dates from them and often commented on the size of women's breasts. They also found a friend of Hill's to whom she had confided about Thomas at the time the harassment took place. There were also other witnesses who corroborated Hill's testimony. These investigators found evidence that supported Hill's claims of Thomas's appetite for pornography.

In October 2007, Hill's guest editorial, "The Smear This Time," appeared in the *New York Times* in response to Clarence Thomas's characterization of her in his memoir, *My Grandfather's Son*.

> ... Justice Thomas has every right to present himself as he wishes in his new memoir, *My Grandfather's Son* ... But I will not stand by silently and allow him, in his anger, to reinvent me.
>
> In the portion of his book that addresses my role in the Senate hearings into his nomination, Justice Thomas offers a litany of unsubstantiated representations and outright smears.... I was a "combative left-winger" who was "touchy" and prone to overreacting to "slights." A number of independent authors have shown those attacks to be baseless. What's more, their reports draw on the experiences of others who were familiar with Mr. Thomas's behavior, and who came forward after the hearings. It's no longer my word against his...

> Justice Thomas's characterization of me is also hobbled by blatant inconsistencies ... In 1981, when Mr. Thomas approached me about working for him, I was an associate in good standing at a Washington law firm ... Yet, Mr. Thomas insists that I was "asked to leave" the firm. Regrettably, since 1991, I have repeatedly seen this kind of character attack on women and men who complain of harassment and discrimination in the workplace ...
>
> Finally, when attacks on the accusers' credibility fail, those accused of workplace improprieties downgrade the level of harm that may have occurred ... to the level of mere words or "slights" that should be dismissed without discussion.
>
> Our legal system will suffer if a sitting justice's vitriolic pursuit of personal vindication discourages others from standing up for their rights.
>
> My hope is that Justice Thomas's latest fusillade will not divert us from that path.[12]

Through it all, Anita Hill relied on her faith as well as the support from her family and friends to see her through. According to Hill, "What ultimately kept me sane was that so much of what was going on was insane. What I had done was the honest, the right, and the correct thing to do."[13]

But it was difficult beyond imagining—devastating, even. Anita Hill deserves the appreciation of every person who has ever or will ever face sexual harassment in the workplace, because despite hostility, threats, attempts at character assassination, and deep personal anguish, she persevered in speaking out against injustice.

Eva Perón: Speaking for Those Without a Voice

> *"Bad moments come, but they go. Some days are fine, some*

> *a little bit harder. But that doesn't mean we should give up our dream."*

Argentina is known for its rich culture, history, sports such as soccer, fine cuisine, music, dance, art ... and the Peróns. Maria Eva Duarte was born out of wedlock in an Argentinean village in 1919. She was the youngest of five children born from the union between a landowner, Juan Duarte, and his cook, Juana Ibarguren.

At the age of seven, Eva lost her father and she witnessed first-hand the struggles her mother faced socially and financially to support the family. She did not want to endure some of the hardships and struggles her mother endured and vowed that her life would be different. As a teenager, she left her family behind and moved to Buenos Aires to pursue her dreams of becoming a movie star. Eva's "profound artistic vocation," as she referred to her calling, was nourished by cinemas in Buenos Aires's Junín district, teenage radio auditions, and her collection of film star pictures. She also had to determine her chosen path as she contemplated whether or not she would follow the course her sisters had taken, the course taken by so many young girls in the town of Junín, or follow her heart and be guided by her own dreams: "Shall I remain a small town girl and marry here as so many girls do? Shall I be a teacher like Blanca? Or an employee like Elisa?"[14] She decided that she would become an actress and would dedicate many years to her passion for the arts. During an interview for the movie magazine *Radiolandia* to discuss her budding career as an actress, she said,

> I am not an adventuress, although some—those who never forgive a young woman for succeeding—make me out to be one. I have spent more than five years dedicated to what is in me a firmly-rooted vocation: the arts. These have been five years of troubles, of noble struggles, when I've known the uncertainty of adversity as well as the gratification of success.[15]

She spent many years touring, working for comedy companies, headlining and starring in stage plays, and taking small parts in films and other productions. Although she did not receive the recognition she felt she deserved, she continued to follow her dreams and her passion for the arts.

Her big break would come when Eva appeared for the first time on the big screen. Opportunities for roles in movies were infrequent; however, she did eventually obtain roles that gave her the visibility she craved. In 1944 she starred in *La cabalgata del circo* and later starred in *La pródiga*, produced in 1945, but never released to the public.

In January 1944, Eva's life would be transformed by her commitment to a cause and, perhaps as important, to a man: Col. Juan Domingo Perón. On January 15, 1944, an earthquake virtually destroyed the Andean city of San Juan and thousands of people died or were left injured. In his capacity as Secretary of Labor and Social Welfare, Perón organized a national relief effort and invited many of Argentina's most popular stars, including Eva, to participate. During the event, Eva and Colonel Perón met and would later begin a relationship. Their budding romance was later confirmed at a gala held at the Colón Opera House on July 9 to celebrate Argentina's Independence Day. Also during this period, Eva was confirmed as president of Agrupación Radial Argentina, a union of radio actors and workers.

Perón's rise to power within the new military government had attracted opposition from his critics; the way he cultivated his relationship with the working classes was distasteful to the Buenos Aires political elite. His relationship with Eva and the powerful role he gave her drew even more criticism; they both became the targets of Perón's opponents. In October 1945, Perón was forced to resign from all his positions. He was detained and sent to Martin Garcia, an island off the coast from Buenos Aires.

However, the workers had realized that Perón's disappearance meant they no longer had a voice in the government; it meant the abandonment of pro-labor policies. On October 17, many workers began abandoning their workplaces and headed towards Plaza de Mayo, demanding the appearance of Perón. Later that night, Perón appeared to announce that elections would be held soon. At that moment, many of the supporters recognized Perón as their leader.

For Eva, the events of these days did not indicate an end, as some had wished, but a new beginning in Argentine history. Perón was eventually chosen as the candidate of the Labor Party. He campaigned all over the country to garner support for his candidacy and his platform. He was accompanied by Eva, who was his strongest supporter and at times campaigned as if she were the candidate running for office. She drummed up support for Perón and even greeted the people personally.

When Perón assumed the Presidency, Eva, or Evita as she was now becoming known, asked herself what role she would assume from then on:

> This is a foundational circumstance and is related directly to my decision to be a president's wife who does not follow the old model. I could have followed those models...
>
> Perón had a double personality and I would need to have one also: I am Eva Perón, the wife of the President, whose work is simple and agreeable ... and I am also Evita, the wife of the leader of a people who have deposited in him all their faith, hope and love. [16]

After Perón became president, Evita undertook her greatest role ever as she took center stage in many causes. She used her voice and position to effect change. She served as a mediator to help solve labor disputes or to help workers obtain better wages. Her relationship with the unions grew in its intensity and became more significant in 1952 as it provided her with her own political platform and political power. She also did humanitarian work for the poor and needy, bringing awareness to their concerns as well as making provision for their emergency needs. Her support among the poor and needy was broadly based, as these groups were often neglected and they were now receiving the attention needed. She increased her visibility among the working class by visiting factories and poor neighborhoods.

She championed the causes of higher wages and greater social welfare benefits as well as state subsidies to assist in the construction of clinics for workers in different industries. She was able to lobby for additional state subsidies to alleviate the suffering of destitute families. She also assisted many poor families in moving from slums outside Buenos Aires to more suitable housing.

As first lady, Eva Perón, the illegitimate child of a landowner, used her very public position to facilitate the inclusion of marginalized groups. She faced opposition from many who benefited from exploiting the powerlessness of marginalized groups; however, the opposition further fueled her passion to be a voice and an advocate for those without a voice. Her passion for "the least of these" helped her to create programs and policies to address and eradicate diseases like tuberculosis and malaria. In 1947, the Maria Eva Duarte De Perón Welfare Foundation was created to help those most in need. Money raised at the Foundation was used to distribute money, food, and medicines to the poor and needy. Reportedly, the money raised in the Foundation came from contributions—not always willingly given—from businesses and unions. The result was very popular with the poor masses, but far less popular with the elite.

Her public position and the support she received from the working class and the poor made her a lightning rod for controversy. One of her most controversial moves was her support of women's suffrage in Argentina. She used her position as first lady to campaign and persuade legislators to give women the right to vote. According to Eva, "Argentine women ... must affirm their action. Women must vote."[17] Her campaigning as well as political and public persuasion gained widespread support and momentum and on September 23, 1947, Law 13.010 was passed, giving women in Argentina the right to vote. Although thrilled with the passage of this important piece of legislation, her work did not stop with the passage of women's suffrage. She actively participated in registering women to vote as well as educating women on the importance of having a voice through voting.

In a visionary—and perhaps overly optimistic—statement, Eva declared in Madrid on June 15, 1947, "This century will not go down in history as the 'Century of World Wars' nor even as the 'Century of Atomic Disintegration,' but rather as the 'Century of Victorious Feminism.'"[18] However, there is no denying the significance of the work she began, which reached beyond Argentina toward neighboring countries and a watching world.

She spearheaded a platform and a political party for women with the founding of the Perónista Women's Party (Partido Perónista Feminino), of which she was elected president. As a result of her efforts, during the 1951 presidential elections, in a move that many described as unprecedented, women were candidates for all the national legislative offices. In addition, according to published reports, 3,816,654 women voted for the first time, resulting in twenty-three female deputies and six female senators joining Congress in 1952.

Eva announced that she would be standing for vice-president in the 1951 election, on the same ticket as Perón. In spite of all the work she did to help move the country forward as well as her many accomplishments among the working class, her candidacy was strongly opposed by the military. Under other circumstances, she would have fought for this position with the same passion and determination with which she fought to help her husband get elected; however, she was diagnosed with cancer and her deteriorating health, combined with the fierce opposition, caused her to decline the nomination.

She died of cancer on July 26, 1952, at the age of 32. Public grief at her death was intense and unprecedented in Argentina. Her precise role in Argentinean politics is still hotly debated, and her supporters and enemies battle it out to write her legacy. There is no doubt, however, that she was a remarkable woman who made her mark on history by using her power and position to make a difference in her beloved country.

Elizabeth Cady Stanton: Silent No More

> *"The moment we begin to fear the opinions of others and hesitate to tell the truth that is in us, and from motives of policy are silent when we should speak, the divine floods of light and life no longer flow into our souls."*

Elizabeth Cady Stanton was born on November 12, 1815, in Johnstown, New York. Her father was a prominent New York attorney who served in the United States Congress for one term. He was also a circuit court judge and a New York Supreme Court justice. Many speculate her love for justice was a result of the many positions held by her father in addition to being introduced to the law by her father at a young age. Her access to her father's law library helped her to see the law from a different perspective in its disproportionately negative effect on women—especially married women. Some accounts suggest that her father's disappointment that she was not a boy had a deep and saddening effect on her childhood. The knowledge and insight Stanton gained from the existing laws was one of the important factors in her determination to work to reform many of those laws as well as to work to gain greater and more equal legal protections for women.

Given her precocious interest in the law as a child, it is perhaps not surprising that Stanton attended coeducational classes at the Johnstown Academy, where she competed successfully with male students in various academic pursuits, winning prizes for her Greek language studies, among other prizes. Simon Hosack, a minister who was also a neighbor of the Cady family during Elizabeth's childhood, encouraged her intellectual development and, indeed, afforded her the sort of parental validation of her pursuits that was denied her by her own father, who in many ways gave her to understand that he valued sons above daughters. Hosack, on the other hand, bequeathed to her a number of books, including a Greek lexicon, from his personal library. Such confirmation of her abilities and aptitude greatly increased Stanton's self-esteem and willingness to think in ways considered unconventional for women in the early and middle nineteenth century.

She was wounded by being denied entry into Union College, which at the time had a males-only admission policy. Thus, she watched in disappointment as many of her former classmates—boys who, in many cases, she surpassed academically—were accepted into the school. This was one of her first experiences with gender discrimination, and it doubtless was a source of her determination to expand the opportunities and protections available to women in American society.

She married Henry Brewster Stanton, an abolitionist, in 1840, and while she had no qualms about taking his surname, she reportedly insisted that the word *obey* be dropped from their marriage ceremony, and she steadfastly refused to refer to herself or be referred to by others as "Mrs. Henry Stanton." To Stanton, this was a diminution of a woman's personhood; she likewise decried the patronizing names by which black men were often known, citing both practices as an evidence of the overbearing attitude prevalent among white males. Though the Stantons differed in their views on a number of issues—including, notably, women's suffrage—Stanton considered their marriage a good one; it lasted forty-seven years, ending with Henry B. Stanton's death in 1887. The Stantons had seven children, and Elizabeth Cady Stanton assumed primary responsibility for their upbringing.

While traveling with her husband to London where he was a

delegate to the World Anti-Slavery Convention, she met Lucretia Mott. Being denied her seat at the convention, as were all the women delegates, Mott discussed with Stanton the inequality faced by American women even as they fought for the rights of other marginalized groups such as slaves. Stanton and Mott discussed the need for a convention on women's rights to address the discrimination against women evidenced by their not being able to speak in London. The idea for a women's convention came to fruition when the two later met in the summer of 1848 in upstate New York. Stanton and Mott, along with other women activists such as Martha Coffin Wright, organized the first women's rights convention, held on July 19 and 20 and attended by more than 300 people. Modeled after the U.S. Declaration of Independence, Stanton's Declaration of Sentiments proposed the then-controversial idea of women's suffrage, declaring that men and women were created equal and should enjoy equality at the polling place and elsewhere. The convention was heavily criticized and ridiculed by the media, church leaders as well as some who viewed women as property and/or felt that women having rights were laughable. After a few amendments, the initial document received some support from approximately one hundred men and women; however, many of the women who initially supported the document later withdrew their support for fear of being ridiculed or stigmatized:

> Philadelphia's *Public Ledger and Daily Transcript* declared that no lady would want to vote. 'A woman is nobody. A wife is everything. The ladies of Philadelphia ... are resolved to maintain their rights as Wives, Belles, Virgins and Mothers.' According to the Albany *Mechanic's Advocate*, equal rights would 'demoralize and degrade [women] from their high sphere and noble destiny ... and prove a monstrous injury to all mankind.[19]

Stanton could have let the negative comments and publicity stop her from fighting for the rights of women; however, being a strategic thinker, she saw the publicity as an opportunity:

> In a letter to Lucretia Mott, she said, 'Imagine the publicity given our ideas by thus appearing in a widely circulated sheet like the *Herald*! It will start women thinking, and men, too.' She drafted lengthy responses to every negative newspaper article and editorial, presenting the reformers' side of the issue to the readers.[20]

Criticism by the media and the responses brought national attention to issues surrounding the rights of women, and many women and even some men were supportive of the issues raised in the document. As a result, many meetings on the rights of women were organized throughout the country and the movement gained momentum. A Declaration of Sentiments and Resolutions was drafted "paraphrasing the Declaration of Independence":

> All men and women are created equal and are endowed by their Creator with certain unalienable rights ... These natural rights belong equally to women and men.[21]

The women also listed and catalogued what they viewed as injustices towards women:

> Women were denied access to higher education, the professions, and the pulpit, as well as equal pay for equal work. If married, they had no property rights; even the wages they earned legally belonged to their husbands. Women were subject to a different moral

> code. Wives could be punished, and in a case of divorce, a mother had no child custody rights.[22]

There were disagreements amongst the women as to which issues the movement should focus their efforts on; Stanton insisted on a broad array of women's issues. Many felt that Stanton's views were too radical, especially her negative opinions of the way women were portrayed in the Old Testament books of the Bible, as well as her disassociation from organized religion. She also began to distance herself from other segments of the feminist movement.

While others, such as Susan B. Anthony, wanted to focus on the single issue of suffrage, Stanton continued to insist that a wider range of topics should be maintained and vigorously championed. This view even led her, on occasion, to engage in racially charged rhetoric, since she believed that enfranchisement of former male slaves would add to the voting population more men who would oppose voting rights for women. However, Stanton ultimately believed in universal suffrage. Also, to the dismay of even some of her liberally minded colleagues such as Susan B. Anthony, Stanton publicly evidenced approval of interracial marriage—a scandalous notion for many at that time.

In spite of the challenges she faced as a child and the opposition and disagreements she had with other feminists about the direction of the women's movement, Stanton spent her life fighting for women's suffrage and equality. She championed, fought for, and won property rights for married women as well as securing their rights to leave marriages where their lives or the lives of their children were in danger or being subjected to abuse. She also spoke out on birth control, taking on an issue that most would not associate with even the most progressive women in nineteenth-century America.

In what would be her final appearance before the United States legislature, Stanton, along with other feminists, testified before the House Judiciary Committee in support of women's suffrage in 1892. In a remarkable life that spanned more than eight decades, she wrote many of the most important speeches, documents, and books of America's first-wave feminist movement. Elizabeth Cady Stanton died in New York on October 26, 1902. Regardless of her various controversial positions, she believed that women should be afforded the same rights as men based on her profound conviction that both men and women were created equal. She died before the 19th Amendment was passed in Congress—the act that gave women the right to vote.

All of these women spoke up in times and under circumstances when it would have been much easier and safer to remain quiet. But despite all the pressures brought to bear on them by societal expectations—in some cases, even in defiance of the laws of the time—they refused to let their voices be stilled. They raised the issues that they believed needed to be raised, and they did it repeatedly and steadfastly, despite opposition that ranged from disapproval to threats of violence. As a result, they changed the world.

In our final look at "misbehaving" women, we will hear stories of those who, through insisting on integrity, brought public scrutiny to bear on unfair and illegal business practices that would undermine and victimize huge swaths of the population. In fact, once women begin to speak out for truth and fairness, there's not much telling where the chips may fall ...

CHAPTER SIX

Insist on Integrity

IN SOME WAYS, FINDING ONE'S VOICE ASSUMES THAT ONE HAS SOMETHING TO SAY. So often in history, when marginalized groups have finally found their voices, it is because they are announcing an uncomfortable truth that the majority or those in power do not want to hear.

Mark Twain is attributed with the saying, "Tell the truth; then you don't have to remember anything." Despite Mark Twain's easy characterization, the past few years of American business history have seen some spectacular lapses in truth-telling. In fact, it seems that as money and power multiply, so does the temptation to play fast and loose with the truth.

In such situations, the stakes are high for those whose integrity will not allow them to remain silent. At the same time, the courage required to listen to that "still, small voice" is indeed great. When large sums of money or great power is at risk, immense pressure is often brought to bear on anyone who raises inconvenient questions or questions the "company line." It is therefore all the more gratifying to know that in the midst of some of the largest financial scandals in recent history, women have risen to the top: women whose inner moral compasses would not permit them to deviate from taking a costly stand for truth and integrity.

Sherron Watkins: Tearing the Lid off Enron

> *"What makes truth uncomfortable? It is uncomfortable when we ignore it, when we suppress it, when we hide from it. Why did so many at Enron keep silent about shoddy accounting practices? Basically, because they got a swift and painful smack to the forehead when they did speak up."*

In 2002, three women won *Time Magazine*'s Persons of the Year. They were dubbed "The Whistleblowers" for their roles in exposing unfair and unlawful activities, shady financial practices, and cover-ups at their respective organizations and agencies. Sherron Watkins and Cynthia Cooper exposed fraudulent financial practices at Enron and WorldCom, respectively, and Coleen Rowley's thirteen-page letter detailed an FBI cover-up of knowledge about terrorist activity in the United States prior to the September 11, 2001, terrorist attacks. By exposing instances where protocol was ignored, questionable record-keeping, and illegal accounting procedures at their organizations, these women took major risks to bring attention to matters that they could not permit to remain hidden beneath a shroud of silence, denial, and deceit.

During the congressional subcommittee hearings into the collapse of Enron, testimony revealed an email from Sherron Watkins, Enron's vice president of corporate development, to chairman Kenneth Lay, warning him that "Enron might implode in a wave of accounting scandals."[1] Her warning proved all too true—with devastating results to thousands of Enron shareholders and especially to Enron employees, many of whom had virtually their total retirement funds invested in Enron stock. When the company did collapse as Watkins predicted, these unfortunate individuals watched their savings disappear, almost overnight.

According to Watkins, she had met with Ken Lay in August 2001 to "warn him of Enron's shady accounting and Lay, for the most part, ignored my warnings." When asked by a reporter what she thought about the verdicts eventually handed down against Lay and other top Enron officials, she said, "My mood [was not] joyous or celebratory. I stammered something about being satisfied that justice prevailed. What I couldn't convey in words is a sense of sadness, sadness for what could have been."[2]

In lamenting "what could have been," Watkins harkened back to the mission statement for the company unveiled in the mid-1990s by Lay and Jeffrey Skilling, Enron's Harvard-trained CEO. No longer would Enron strive to be "The World's Leading Energy Company," leadership declared. According to Watkins, "We were going to be 'The World's Leading Company.' Why limit ourselves to energy?"[3]

"Enron was fast-paced, inventive, exciting," Watkins said. "We epitomized the New Economy: able to innovate virtually overnight."[4] Unfortunately, in life, our strengths can become our weaknesses. Just as the dark side of charisma is narcissism, the dark side of innovation is fraud—Enron fell victim to both.

Watching Sherron Watkins during the hearings and trying to understand the pain in her eyes as the company she loved began to self-destruct, I remembered having many similar feelings while working for an organization that had fallen on tough times. I connected emotionally with Watkins because we both belonged to organizations with mission statements that resonated deeply within us. These organizations had all the ingredients to be great organizations and leaders in their industries.

Unfortunately, we all know what happens with the presence of a few bad apples. As became apparent with Enron, when the bad apples are the leaders, those who literally hold the keys to the future of the organization in the palm of their hands, the results can be disastrous. Ironically, we often find that many of these leaders graduated from the best colleges and universities, sometimes at the top of their classes.

Certainly, many corporate leaders earn their way to the top

because of hard work and dedication; however, when they get there, they sometimes prove unable to handle the pressure to perform, to deliver what is expected of them. Others want to win at all costs, to maintain their competitive edge, and they begin to cut corners, ultimately resulting in the very sort of spectacular failure they were hoping to avoid.

We want our leaders to be honest, we want them to be intelligent, and we want them to be just. In short, we expect them to possess the qualities that exemplify great leaders. However, all too many leaders are narcissistic, self-absorbed, and intolerant of ideas other than their own. Unlike Enron's Kenneth Lay, they are not always polished nor are they always charismatic. Sometimes having received a job because of whom they know, their race, or their gender; they are actually incompetent to lead, having neither the courage nor the intellect. Instead, they resort to fear and intimidation. Because of their lack of experience or expertise, they feel threatened by anyone who questions their decisions or authority. Without the positional authority granted by their job descriptions, such individuals couldn't lead a fly to honey, in most cases.

I recall, as a new hire at a particular organization, asking the boss what advice he would give to new employees. He responded, "Just do your job to the best of your ability and do it with integrity." I liked that; his words resonated with me. I also liked that he spoke about integrity in a way that indicated he valued it above all else. He also stated that he preferred to work with people who were loyal.

As I got to know him, however, and as I observed some of his business and management practices, I realized that he would, in fact, sell his mother if that would help him get ahead. I witnessed this man altering documents, telling outright lies, and stealing ideas and work created by his colleagues and subordinates and then presenting it as his own.

During a meeting, this individual mentioned to me that he did not believe we had a connection; he felt that he had a hard time engaging me. I thought for a minute before I responded: first, because his comments took me aback; and second, because I am not known for mincing words, and I wanted to be careful how I answered. I asked him if he wanted to hear the truth and he said, "no." However, I proceeded to tell him what I thought, anyway. I related how, at our first meeting, I was excited to work with him because of what he told me about integrity and loyalty; however, I said that I didn't believe he practiced what he preached.

He told me that if I liked my job, I would keep my opinion to myself, then basically dismissed me from his presence. A few hours later, I received an email from my manager who wanted to talk to me about my attitude and having respect for those in authority.

Clearly, Sherron Watkins had a difficult choice to make as she began to discover some of the improper accounting techniques that were being used to keep the truth about Enron's finances from showing up in its annual reports. There is little question that she was very familiar with the egos of her superiors in the organization. She also likely knew about their practice of responding aggressively and sometimes with hostility to any outside analyst or critic who expressed doubts about Enron's financial underpinnings or long-term viability. On one occasion, for example, during a recorded conference call, a Wall Street analyst wondered aloud why Enron couldn't provide a balance sheet along with its earnings statements, like every other publicly traded company. CEO Skilling's response was to call the analyst an asshole.

If Enron's leadership would stoop to such disrespect toward someone outside the organization, Sherron Watkins must have had serious misgivings about what they might do to someone in "the Enron family" who raised public doubts about the company. Nevertheless, she dutifully wrote her fateful email to her boss, laying out point by point the financial skeletons in Enron's closet that were just waiting to be discovered by disgruntled investors and employees who were being slowly roasted alive by Enron's falling stock price. When she hit "send" on the email, what did she feel? Perhaps more to the point, how did she feel when nearly every one of the points raised in her warning came true—with devastating results?

Sherron Watkins had the courage to face what the leaders of her company refused to acknowledge. In other words, Enron fell victim to an appalling lapse in leadership integrity. And, in difficult economic times such as those in place as I write this, it is more imperative than ever that organizations—and the public they serve—demand the highest standards in leadership.

Companies look at their turnover rates and wonder why they are having a hard time retaining key talent. As an HR professional, I know first-hand that they spend a lot of money on surveys to find out how to engage and retain their employees. And yet, inexplicably, they turn a blind eye to poor leadership and lapses in integrity. I have personally witnessed too many instances of companies being aware that tyrants are parading as leaders, but who seem to believe that if they look the other way, the problem will vanish. Likewise, organizations spend a lot of money to revise and implement new policies, but when it comes time to enforce the policies, they acquiesce to bad leadership behavior.

When leaders fail to act internally, employees will often react externally. Like Sherron Watkins, employees with integrity will be able to tolerate only so much before their limit is reached and the formerly internal problem becomes uncomfortably public. The question being posed by the Sherron Watkinses of the world is this: Will we learn from the Enron lesson in leadership failures, or will we just shrug our shoulders and thank God we're not Ken Lay?

Noreen Harrington: Exposing Unfair Trading on Wall Street

> *"I knew I needed to tell somebody, just so I could sleep with what I knew."*

Described by some as a "reluctant hero," a few years after the

Enron scandal, Noreen Harrington placed an anonymous call to New York State Attorney General Eliot Spitzer about trading irregularities at the Wall Street firm where she worked.

Like Lilly Ledbetter, Harrington did not set out to be a trailblazer or a household name. She was not examining every little practice or procedure for incidents of fraud and wrongdoing within her organization. She was a good hard worker who did her job—and did it well. She was also a capable and competent employee with over two decades of experience working for some of the top firms on Wall Street. In 1997 she was named one of the top 50 women in finance according to *Euromoney*, a trade magazine.

Known as late trading, the practice flagged by Harrington involves completing trades after the market is closed for the day and sending in orders hours after the 4:00 p.m. deadline based on information about whether the market is going to go up or down. It is an illegal practice and investors can lose money as a result. Harrington found out about the practice from colleagues who bragged about the money they made as a result of this unlawful procedure.

According to Harrington, she made the anonymous call to the attorney general's office because she wanted to clear her conscience. "I knew I needed to tell somebody, just so I could sleep..." She also said that she did not tell anyone about making the anonymous call because the situation was scary: "I told nobody. These are powerful people. And some [of them] are going to go to jail ... I called because I thought I was a witness to a crime."[5] She could have decided that it wasn't worth the hassle and harassment that would inevitably come with being labeled a whistleblower. Harrington's decision to come forward was not an easy decision. She reportedly wrestled with the decision before realizing that people she knew were victims of the fraud,

> My sister is one of the hardest workers I know. Suddenly I saw her as a victim of this crime. Up

> until then, I hadn't really thought about the human toll: all those Americans whose only liquid asset is their 401(k). And after I looked at it from the bottom up, then I couldn't sleep at night. I knew I had to call somebody.[6]

When asked about her decision to come forward, Harrington says,

> No one wants to be a whistle-blower. No one dreams as a little child, 'I hope one day I grow up to be a whistle-blower.' Certainly, I did not. I was an industry insider. I worked at prestigious firms, including Goldman, Sachs & Co. and Barclays Capital. I was successful in my career. Why would I want to jeopardize everything? Certainly, it can turn a person's life upside down...[7]

As a result of Harrington blowing the whistle, the attorney general's office brought several criminal charges against the funds and traders in question. Those found guilty agreed to repay investors for the money they lost. Harrington was instrumental in bringing attention to a practice that, though illegal, was so subtle it had gone unnoticed. However, she paid attention to what was being said in her work environment and realized that something was not right. She trusted her instincts and took action when she realized that a crime was being committed.

As noted earlier, the first decade of the twenty-first century has had more than its share of whistleblowers who happen to be women. When asked about this trend, then–New York Attorney General Eliot Spitzer stated, "By definition, women aren't part of the old boys' network. And somehow the old boys' network has generated this notion of, 'Don't tell anybody what we're doing.' Women who have begun to succeed are rising through the ranks and are saying to themselves, 'Wait a minute, you're doing what?'"[8] Spitzer's comments are confirmed by studies showing that women tend to act more ethically than men.

Many whistleblowers of both genders have jeopardized their careers and, in some cases, their lives by coming forward to bring attention to issues that are illegal or irregular. Many have gone on to lead somewhat normal lives in spite of the stigma society sometimes attaches to whistleblowers. However, some report trouble finding work within the same industry. Others have written books, gone on the lecture circuit, or seen their experience utilized as case studies for ethics courses in universities and in-house corporate training.

Coming forward and taking a stand for integrity is not for the faint of heart. Whistleblowers are often shunned, may lose their jobs, and are usually blacklisted so that they have trouble finding employment within the same or a different industry. If you are a single parent or the main breadwinner in your family, the loss in income may be particularly difficult to contemplate. No one—at least initially—likes a whistleblower. Many of the women who became known as whistleblowers filed complaints through company channels that were ignored. Some feared for their safety before and after coming forward.

By taking a stand and doing what she knew was right, Harrington sparked an investigation that exposed illegal trading practices on Wall Street—resulting in many organizations reviewing their practices and their policies on ethics. She strongly dislikes the term whistle-blower, "If you stop on the side of the road and you help somebody that's in trouble, you're a Good Samaritan but if I try to reach out to help small investors I'm a whistle-blower."[9]

Coleen Rowley: Revealing Another Tragedy of 9/11

"Loyalty to whomever you work for is extremely important. The only problem is, it's not the most important thing. And

when it comes to not admitting mistakes, or covering up or not rectifying things only to save face, that's a problem."

Coleen Rowley's love of the FBI began decades before she joined the agency as a special agent. One of her favorite television shows was *The Man from U.N.C.L.E.* Not realizing the show was fiction, she wrote a letter to the producers of the show asking how she might join the ranks of "supersecret spies."

According to Rowley, she received a letter from the show's producers. "They said U.N.C.L.E. didn't exist. But they told me that in the United States, we had something called the FBI. And they gave me the address." Determined to follow her passion, Rowley wrote a letter to the FBI and they sent her a pamphlet titled, "99 Facts About the FBI." One of the questions was, "Does the FBI employ women as special agents?" The answer was no. "I thought to myself, 'That's stupid,'" Rowley said. "I figured that would change eventually."[10] It did change, and in January 1981, she was appointed as a special agent with the FBI.

After the September 11, 2001, terrorist attacks, the public outcry was enormous and Americans everywhere wanted answers from our leaders and our government: How could this horrible act happen on our soil? Why weren't we protected? Why did so many die? Why, with perhaps the best intelligence organization in the world, was our country unable to foresee this attack?

While the public demanded answers, there were many within our intelligence agencies—the CIA and FBI—who wanted answers as well: especially those who were aware of terrorist activities prior to the attack. For example, how was it possible that the terrorists responsible for the attacks were taking flight lessons and that the intelligence community was unaware of it?

Coleen Rowley was most confused and had her own questions. She carried around the burden of knowing that in some way, her agency had failed the very people they took an oath to protect. Why had the agency failed to adequately heed the warnings in the case of Zacarias Moussaoui, a French-Moroccan who had signed up at a local flight school and expressed an interest in 747s? There is no clear evidence that the information that was brought to the attention of Rowley's superiors would have stopped the attacks of September 11; however, there is also no clear evidence that it would not have helped or that it might not have been useful toward a greater effort to prevent the attacks.

Recognizing what she saw as a cover-up within her own agency, Rowley decided to write a letter to FBI Director Robert Mueller. Prior to writing the letter, she considered the cost. At the time, she was the sole breadwinner for her family and did not have any other sources of income. In addition, she recognized that she would raise a few eyebrows and probably face reprimand or termination for ignoring the chain of command and addressing her issues directly to Mueller rather than to her immediate superiors. However, Rowley concluded that the FBI was more concerned about protecting its image and reputation than protecting the public.

Comments made by Mueller after the September 11 attacks caught Rowley and her colleagues by surprise. Mueller publicly stated, "The fact that there were a number of individuals that happened to have received training at flight schools here is news, quite obviously." Mueller further stated, "There were no warning signs that I'm aware of that would indicate this type of operation in the country."[11] As a result of the comments, Rowley decided to act on her convictions.

She wrote a thirteen-page scathing letter to Mueller detailing the FBI's lack of response "to evidence of terrorist activity in the United States prior to September 11th."[12] Concerned about the impact the letter might have on her livelihood, Rowley added language in the letter regarding protections she was entitled to under the Whistleblower Protection Act of 1989, which protects federal employees from retaliation for reporting crimes, corruption, and errors made within federal agencies.

According to Rowley, shortly after mailing the letter, she received a call from CNN asking her about the letter. Confused as to the unfolding events and apprehensive because of an apparent leak to the media, Rowley denied having any knowledge of the letter. The contents of the letter, however, ignited a firestorm of controversy, and the leaks and the subsequent publicity thrust upon Rowley and others from her office eventually led to being called to testify about what they knew before the House and Senate Intelligence Committees joint inquiry into the attacks of September 11, 2001.

Many praised Rowley for her courage in writing the letter as well as testifying publicly about the events leading up to the September 11 attacks. Even though her job was protected under the Whistleblower Protection Act, she ultimately committed career suicide. According to Rowley, there were reports of criminal charges against her that were being discussed by her superiors. Retired FBI agents felt that she was disloyal. Many of these agents cited an old loyalty essay from Elbert Hubbard that graced the walls of the FBI headquarters while J. Edgar Hoover headed the agency:

> If you work for a man, in heaven's name, work for him; speak well of him and stand by the institution he represents. Remember—an ounce of loyalty is worth a pound of cleverness ... If you must growl, condemn, and eternally find fault, why, resign your position, and when you are on the outside, damn to your heart's content.[13]

Rowley reported receiving many copies of this essay, accompanied by requests for her to resign her position. She further stated, "It wasn't even anonymous! They signed their names!"[14]

Rowley felt strongly that she did the right thing; however, she was hurt by the way her actions were viewed and how she was treated. I can only imagine how Rowley felt when she came forward to do what she believed was right, only to have those whom she looked up to and whose opinions she strongly valued turn against her. As a child, she had dreamed of becoming part of the FBI during a time when women were not yet allowed to join the agency. Indeed, she won an award in 1984 for her work in a nationally publicized case and received recognition for her work on several other high-profile cases. She could have looked the other way to protect an agency that had allowed her to fulfill her childhood dream; she could have turned a blind eye to the agency's failures and considered a team player. However, she ultimately decided she could no longer carry the burden of what she knew. She wrote a letter as a way of calling attention to broken policies and bad protocol at the FBI.

Clearly, she was fearful of the backlash and understood she might be committing career suicide—and events proved her fears well founded. As an American impacted by the terrorist attacks of September 11, she had to bring attention to the problem not only to expose the cover-up but also to do what she could to make sure that future attacks did not happen without warning. Responding to her critics who implied that her gender was the reason for her memo, Rowley denied any association between gender and doing the right thing. According to Rowley, "There are plenty of women who have been co-opted, who don't do the right thing. And there are plenty of men who do."[15]

Marlene Braun: Despair and Tragedy

> *"I … can't keep fighting indefinitely, I don't think … [but m]aybe fighting is better than capitulating…."*

Indeed, for those who contemplate bringing to light matters that their organizations would prefer to keep concealed, it is vital to carefully consider the cost and know clearly what is at stake. In some cases, the ensuing harassment, opposition, and character assassination that is carried out in order to attempt to discredit a whistleblower can become too much to bear. The case of Marlene Braun provides a sad example.

Marlene Braun worked for the U.S. Bureau of Land Management for nearly thirteen years. She was appointed manager of Carrizo Plain National Monument: 250,000 acres of native grasses and sites sacred in Native American culture. During the George W. Bush administration, Interior Secretary Gale Norton was in the process of crafting a grazing policy that lifted protections for wildlife and habitat across 161 million acres of public lands in the West. Braun disagreed with her new bosses on these policies, believing that the administration's pro-grazing policies would have negative impact on the fragile bioregion encompassed by the Carrizo Plain National Monument. When Braun voiced her disagreement, she felt she was stripped of "almost all my influence on the Plain," influence that was transferred to those she deemed to be "pro-grazing." She repeatedly clashed with her bosses and wrote to colleagues, "I ... can't keep fighting indefinitely, I don't think ... [but m]aybe fighting is better than capitulating.... The Carrizo could lose a lot if I give up ... But hell, you only live, and die, once!"[16]

Braun took her concerns to other officials at the Department of Fish and Game as well as notifying the Nature Conservancy about "several public misstatements she believed [her boss] had made about federal grazing law." When her supervisor found out, he suspended her. She immediately appealed her suspension; however, her appeal was denied. Braun continued to address her issues and displeasure with officials regarding the Carrizo Plain and was disciplined and reprimanded as a result.[17]

She shared with those close to her that she believed she could be fired as a result of her continuous complaining to officials. Nevertheless, Braun felt a deeply personal commitment to the ecological well-being of the Carrizo Plain National Monument that would not allow her to acquiesce to policies that she considered fundamentally wrong for the environment. Accordingly, she continued registering complaints and forwarding to officials at the

Department of Fish and Game and the Nature Conservancy the disciplinary memos she continued to receive.

In the end, the pressure became too much for her, the uphill battle too long and wearying. She wrote, "I will no longer be participating in this mess ... I will not take being treated like a whipping girl..." The day after writing this, she put a .38 caliber pistol to her head and pulled the trigger.[18]

Braun's suicide was a complete tragedy on so many levels that it garnered national attention. The outcry from her friends, family, conservationists as well as complete strangers resulted in a federal investigation that led to the transfer of her supervisor. Many of Braun's concerns were addressed as a result of the investigation—operating procedures were reviewed and new policies and procedures were either revised or created to help protect the Carrizo Plain.

While many of the circumstances surrounding Braun's suicide remain unknown, it seems clear that she reached the point of feeling unable to continue living with the impossible position she was in. It is certainly a tragedy that Braun reached such an impasse in trying to achieve redress of her concerns that she came to feel that suicide was the only way out.

Once again, however, I am reminded that it is necessary to consider the cost. By refusing to acquiesce, I lost a job. Braun lost her life. Multitudes of others have faced criticism, harassment, firing, and even death threats as a result of refusal to remain quiet in the face of dishonesty. There may indeed be times when it is better to walk away if you feel your health and well-being are in jeopardy. Support groups and employee assistance programs may also be available to help you cope with the grief and depression that may be brought on by integrity issues and other stressors in the workplace.

Another sad lesson that might be learned from the life and death of Braun is that when hope dies, life seems not worth living. In fact, in order to have the sort of inner strength needed to stand up to the forces that are inevitably arrayed against them, "misbehaving" women throughout history have often relied on faith and their convictions: in God, in themselves, in their cause, or in the future they were trying to provide for those who came after them. For these women, that inner bastion sustained them even in the times when it seemed the entire world was attempting to tear them down.

And so, as we conclude this journey, as we allow the stories of these women to find their places within us, it is time to end as we began: with the importance of faith.

CHAPTER SEVEN

Keep Holding on to Your Faith

WITH THIS CHAPTER, WE COME FULL CIRCLE, BACK TO THE PLACE WHERE WE began: the importance of faith—the foundation from which our core values and convictions stem. Faith is what sustains us when nothing else will; it keeps hope alive even when everything around us seems hopeless.

Remember: You Matter!

Throughout most of history, women have been told, in open and unspoken ways, that they were important primarily for performing the roles defined for them by males: conceiving and bearing children, keeping the household, and catering to the needs and desires of their men. For women who presumed to step outside these roles or to seek their significance in ways that the surrounding society didn't sanction, disapproval was certain and punishment likely. Women who were determined to follow their own paths had to find their own, inner sources of validation and significance—society certainly wasn't going to hand either to them!

In the same way today, if we, as women of ambition and vision, are serious about seeking self-definition and rejecting the ready-made roles that society seeks to force on us, we must be able to remind ourselves that we matter—even when everything and everyone around is trying to tell us we don't!

The great cathedrals of Europe were built by artisans and laborers who, even in their own lifetimes, were virtually anonymous. A stonecutter would work his entire life to shape and place the stones that would form the walls, columns, and buttresses of these magnificent structures. He would grow old and die, often passing his trade and his role in the construction on to his son. That son, in his turn, might grow old in his labor and pass the mantle to his son who might, if he lived long enough, actually live to see the completion of the cathedral that contained stones laid by his father and grandfather.

Even though most of those who labored diligently to build and beautify the cathedrals might never see the fruits of their work, and even though their names are, in the vast majority of cases, lost in the dust of centuries, their work remains to this day. What they did was important, even though their names have been forgotten. In many ways, theirs was a work of faith—they adhered steadfastly to the tasks they were given, even though they knew that they were not likely to see the end results for which they labored.

In many ways, this is similar to the situation of "misbehaving" women today: they must persist in faith, believing that what they do is important—that it makes a difference. The short-term benefits may be difficult to discern, but women of vision must continue on, firm in the inner knowledge that what is most popular or most visible may not always be what is most important.

A Higher Power than Ourselves

In the Christian scriptures, there is a verse that says, "If God is for us, who can be against us?" (Romans 8:31). I interpret this verse to mean, among other things, that there is a higher power that is greater than the powers that may be opposing me at a given time.

Whether your faith is based in the teachings of one of the world's great religions, in a belief in the power of the human spirit, on a hope for a better future for your children, or on any other source, trusting this higher power and calling upon it in times of difficulty is central to remaining true to your inner vision. In my darkest times, when I had no allies in sight, I was able to draw upon the lessons of my faith and realize that the Power that shaped my future was still in control, was still firmly welded into the depths of my soul, and was still sustaining me as I tried to make sense of my situation.

Without exception, the women profiled in this book have been through similar times, facing, in some cases, far greater trials than you or I may ever be called to face. And yet, each of them found the inner will to continue on, to believe that her vision was true, that her dreams mattered, and that she could, in fact, take the next step. As you embark upon this journey, you, too, must look within yourself and find your place of inner strength, recognizing that its origins are in a place that is beyond the troubles of the moment.

You Can't Live without Hope

As I stated at the beginning of the book, faith is the single most essential element for any person who is seeking to change the world—or even change her own life. Without faith—and the hope it inspires—we have no incentive to lift our vision above whatever good or bad circumstances we may be dealing with. Without the belief that things could be different than they were, Sojourner Truth would never have left her master and embarked on the road to freedom and self-determination. Without hope, Rahab would never have turned her face away from Jericho and toward her new and better future with the Israelites. Without hope, Betty Friedan would never have chronicled the malaise of women in mid–twentieth-century America, giving them a voice and defining a movement that continues to this day. Without hope, in other words, there is no reason to try. Without hope, nothing changes.

In his unforgettable book *One Yellow Daffodil*, David Adler illustrates the power of faith. The book's main character, Morris Kaplan, is a Holocaust survivor who, because of the horrors of his experiences, has left his faith behind. However, one year, he is invited to the home of two of his young customers, Jonathan and Ilana, for their Hanukkah celebration. During the course of the evening, he finds himself retelling his experiences at Auschwitz as a young child. He remembers that there was a single yellow daffodil that grew in the mud of the camp, and that each day he would look carefully at that flower, the only beautiful thing he could find amid all the brutality and ugliness. Morris is eventually rescued from the camp and immigrates to the United States. He grows up and becomes the owner of a flower shop. By the end of the book, he realizes that despite the horrendous things he witnessed and experienced at Auschwitz, that one yellow daffodil kept his hope alive. And because of that, he is now ready to allow faith back into his heart. By remembering both the horror and the hope, Morris Kaplan is, in a sense, reborn. Such is the power of faith—the power of hope.

Teaching Our Daughters, Molding Our Sons

One of the most important things we can do as we learn the stories of women who have made a difference is pass those stories on to our children—our daughters, sons, nephews, nieces, and all the other young people in our lives. That, in fact, is the principal power of stories: by passing them on, we multiply their power and their capacity to change the way people think.

We teach our daughters that they can be anything they want to be; however, we must also teach them how to deal with and respond to real-life sexism. Likewise, we must teach our sons to respect women as fellow human beings who are capable of doing and being anything they set their minds to. By introducing our children to the stories of these women, and to similar stories of others who have fought for the rights that we often take for granted, we can instill in them both an appreciation for how difficult it has been, in many cases, for us to arrive at the place we are now, and also an expectation that they will grow into people who will be part of the solution, not part of the problem.

Our society desperately needs strong men who have the

self-confidence and sensitivity to listen carefully to each person, regardless of gender, race, ethnicity, or any other differentiating factor, and respect their uniqueness and the validity of their ideas. Our society needs strong women who know who they are and who are confident in their ability to act on their dreams and ambitions, unfettered by limitations based on preconceived notions of "proper" roles for women. It is our responsibility as parents and mentors to help our children and young friends become these sorts of men and women. And in order to do that, the stories must become a part of their emotional and intellectual heritage.

And we must go further; we must become the people that we want our children to be. It isn't enough to simply know the stories of the "misbehaving" women who have changed the world. We must do everything we can, in our own day, to incorporate their stories into our own—to put flesh and bone on the words and ideas, and to demonstrate for our children that change, determination, dreams, and persistence are not just something that people in history have had, but something we possess, and something that has to be part of their daily experience, as well.

By helping our children incorporate these stories into their lives and actions and by living them ourselves, we are reaffirming the importance of role models. Just as Nelson Mandela in his prison cell was inspired by and strove to emulate Gandhi, so we can find inspiration and strength by contemplating the struggles and ultimate victories of women like Susan B. Anthony, Rosa Parks, Anita Hill, and Golda Meir.

If we can become inspired ourselves, then we can inspire our children. By living in front of them what it means to listen to our own voices, to pursue our own paths, to rise above externally imposed limitations, and to do it all while holding onto the central core of our belief, we can build into their minds the expectation that they can live this way, too. And by doing this, we can create a mechanism for a transformation in the lives of women and men for generations to come.

A Better Path

And now the path lies before you. This is the story I wanted to tell you, the story I needed to hear myself. I began seeking it out during a time of personal upheaval, as I tried to make sense of suddenly being out of a job, derailed from a career, and deprived of the opportunity to do work in which I deeply believed. I hope that you are not in such a place as you read these words. But if you are, take heart. Be encouraged in the knowledge that generations of women have experienced some or all of what you are dealing with, and have still managed to triumph.

By beginning from a place of faith, and by holding onto your faith no matter what happens in your life, you will have the basis for hope, the one truly indispensable quality for life. Your hope will then empower you to choose your own path, not on the basis of avoiding discomfort or conforming to some external standard, but based instead on what you believe in the deepest parts of your being. As you move out along the path you have chosen, you will begin to rise above the limitations others will seek—either subconsciously or purposefully—to place on you. You will be able to resist the opposition that is sure to arise, recognizing it for what it is: an attempt by those who lack courage, vision, or sensitivity to protect a status quo that they perceive as necessary to their own well-being.

As you steadfastly continue your journey, you will notice that you are not the only one who is being opposed or stigmatized by unjust expectations and unfair systems. This is the part of the journey where you must find your voice in order to oppose injustice, to speak out against oppression that seeks to limit your pursuit of your destiny. You will find as you do this that justice and integrity are inextricably related, and you will understand that you must insist on integrity in yourself and in all those around you. By living your life with integrity, you will come to realize that this is the key to becoming the person you were intended to be.

And, all along the way, you must continue to protect the place of faith in your life. You must nurture your spirit and remain firmly connected to that place deep within you that is the anchor point for your strength and your hope. By doing that, you will add to a life of accomplishment the most important thing of all—meaning.

I hope that the stories in this book have inspired you. I hope that by learning about some of the accomplishments of "misbehaving" women throughout history, you have drawn encouragement for your own journey. One of the greatest things about stories like these, as I have said, is the way they get inside us, reshaping the ways we think, feel, and act. In that sense, these stories are unfinished; each of us writes a continuation of the stories as we live out their principles in our lives and as we pass them on to others.

I would love to hear your stories. If you would like to share a victory, a struggle, or simply a quiet moment of realization that came to you as you traveled the path toward your dreams, please get in touch with me at www.dawnnicolemartin.com or dawn@dawnnicolemartin.com. I hope you'll add your own threads to the growing tapestry being created by women of courage and vision, women who have decided to pursue their own dreams and demand that their voices be heard ... women who dare to misbehave.

Sources Consulted

Bible quotations are taken from *Conparative Study Bible,* Revised Edition. Grand Rapids, MI: Zondervan, 1999.

Introduction: All My Life I Had to Fight

1. Franklin, Kirk. "My Life Is In Your Hands." *God's Property.* Cond. Kirk Franklin. Comp. Kirk Franklin. 2. 1997. Compact Disc.
2. Walker, Alice. *The Color Purple.* 1st Edition. Orlando, FL: Harcourt Brace Jovanovich, 1982.
3. Ulrich, Laurel Thatcher. *Well-Behaved Women Seldom Make History.* New York, NY: Knopf, 2007.
4. Harrison, Kathryn. "Sunday Book Review: We're No Angels." *New York Times*, September 30, 2007.
5. Kennedy, Edward M. *Senator Edward M. Kennedy's eulogy of his brother, Robert F. Kennedy.* June 8, 1968. http://www.jfklibrary.org/Asset-Viewer/5NP_WJXjD0aKKslRuO6-sw.aspx (accessed March 30, 2011).

Chapter 1: Hold Onto Your Faith

1. Franklin, Kirk. "My Life Is In Your Hands." *God's Property.* Cond. Kirk Franklin. Comp. Kirk Franklin. 2. 1997. Compact Disc.

Chapter 2: Choose Your Own Course

1. Pogrebin, Letty Cottin. "Golda Meir." *Jewish Women: A Comprehensive Historical Encyclopedia.* Edited by Jewish Women's Archive. March 20, 2009. http://jwa.org/encyclopedia/article/meir-golda (accessed June 17, 2010).

2. Ibid.
3. Ibid.
4. Shenker, Israel. "Golda Meir: Peace and Arab Acceptance Were Goals of Her 5 Years as Premier." *New York Times.* December 9, 1978. http://www.nytimes.com/learning/general/onthisday/bday/0503.html (accessed June 12, 2010).
5. Pogrebin, Letty Cottin. "Golda Meir." *Jewish Women: A Comprehensive Historical Encyclopedia.* Edited by Jewish Women's Archive. March 20, 2009. http://jwa.org/encyclopedia/article/meir-golda (accessed June 17, 2010).
6. Ibid.
7. Ibid.
8. Reed, Susan. "Storming the Citadel: Firing the Loudest Shots in Charleston Since the Assault on Fort Sumter, Shannon Faulkner Attacks the Gender Barrier at a Venerable Military School." *People Magazine*, 24 1994, January: 44–46.
9. Bennett-Haigney, Lisa. *Faulkner Makes History at the Citadel.* August 1995. http://www.now.org/nnt/08-95/citadel.html (accessed June 12, 2010).
10. *Faulkner v. Jones.* 51 F.3d 440 (UNITED STATES DISTRICT COURT FOR THE DISTRICT OF SOUTH CAROLINA, CHARLESTON DIVISION, July 22, 1994).
11. Sack, Kevin. "A Woman Reports for Duty As a Cadet at The Citadel." *The New York Times*, August 13, 1995.
12. Janofsky, Michael. "Citadel, Bowing to Court, Says It Will Admit Women." *The New York Times*, June 29, 1996.
13. Bennett-Haigney. "New Fronts in The Citadel Battle." *National NOW Times*, November 1995. http://www.now.org/nnt/11-95/shannon.html (accessed June 12, 2010).
14. Faulkner, Shannon, interview by JUJU CHANG. "Life After the Citadel: Shannon Faulkner Reflects on Her Historic Battle with the Elite Military College." *Good Morning America.* ABC News. New York. December 8, 2009.
15. Biography.com. *Biography.com.* 2009. http://www.biography.com/articles/Sarah-Palin-360398 (accessed June 12, 2010).
16. Palin, Sarah. "2008 US Presidential Elections." *Republican National Convention: Sarah Palin's Acceptance Speech.* September 1–4, 2008.
17. Stephanoupoulos, George, and Ed O'Keefe. "McCain Taps Alaska Governor Palin as Vice Presidential Running Mate State's First Female

Governor Brings Youth, Conservative Appeal to GOP Ticket." *CNN.com*. August 29, 2008.

18. Palin, Sarah, interview by Oprah Winfrey. "Going Rogue." *The Oprah Show.* Harpo Studios. Chicago. November 16, 2009.
19. Ibid.
20. Ibid.
21. Palin, Sarah. *Going Rogue: An American Life.* New York, NY: HarperCollins, 2009.
22. Hopkins, Kyle. "Gov. Palin gives birth to son Trig (04/18/08)." *Anchorage Daily News*, April 18, 2008.
23. Palin, Sarah. *Going Rogue: An American Life.* New York, NY: HarperCollins, 2009.
24. Clinton, Hillary Rodham. *Living History.* New York, NY: Simon & Schuster, 2003.
25. Clinton, Hillary, interview by Soledad O'Brien. "Sojourners Presidential Forum." *The Situation Room: Special Edition.* CNN. Washington. June 4, 2007.
26. Ibid.
27. Douglas, Susan J. *Where The Girls Are: Growing Up Female with the Mass Media.* New York, NY: Three Rivers Press, 1995.
28. LaSalle, Mick. *Complicated Women: Sex and Power in Pre-Code Hollywood.* New York, NY: Martin Press, 2001.
29. Biography.com. *Biography of Mae West.* http://www.maewest.nl/biografie2.html (accessed September 2010, 2010).
30. Ibid.
31. Ibid.
32. Ibid.
33. Charlton, Linda. *On This Day: Assassination in India-A Leader of Will and Force; Indira Gandhi, Born to Politics, Left Her Own Imprint on India.* http://www.nytimes.com/learning/general/onthisday/bday/1119.html (accessed June 7, 2010).
34. Ibid.
35. Kunin, Madeline M. *Women Leaders: Indira Gandhi's Legacy.* May 3, 2008. http://www.theglobalist.com/StoryId.aspx?StoryId=6981 (accessed December 17, 2009).
36. Thatcher, Margaret. *Speech to Conservative Party Conference ('the lady's not for turning').* October 10, 1980. http://www.margaretthatcher.org/document/104431 (accessed August 21, 2010).

Chapter 3: Rise Above Limitations

1. "Seneca Falls Convention." West's Encyclopedia of American Law. 2005. *Encyclopedia.com.* http://www.encyclopedia.com/doc/1G2-3437703977.html (accessed March 7, 2010).
2. Mabee, Carleton, and Mabee Newhouse, Susan. *Sojourner Truth: Slave, Prophet, Legend* . New York, NY: NYU Press, 1993.
3. PBS. "Betty Friedan Interview." *PBS.org.* http://www.pbs.org/fmc/interviews/friedan.htm (accessed March 7, 2010).
4. Friedan, Betty. *The Feminine Mystique.* New York, NY: W. W. Norton & Company, 2001.
5. PBS. "Betty Friedan Interview." *PBS.org.* http://www.pbs.org/fmc/interviews/friedan.htm (accessed March 7, 2010).
6. National Organization for Women. "The National Organization for Women's 1966 Statement of Purpose." *National Organization for Women (NOW).* October 29, 1966. http://www.now.org/history/purpos66.html?printable (accessed March 17, 2010).
7. Cronkite, Walter. "The Announcement, The Strategy, and In Context." *Campaign '72.* January 25, 1972. http://www.chisholm72.net/campaign.html (accessed March 21, 2010).
8. Chisholm, Shirley. *The Good Fight (A Cass Canfield Book).* New York, NY: HarpersCollins, 1973.
9. Lamb, Yvonne Shinhoster. *Pioneering Politician, Advocate Shirley Chisholm Dies.* January 24, 2005. http://www.washingtonpost.com/wp-dyn/articles/A46322-2005Jan4.html (accessed March 8, 2010).
10. Chisholm, Shirley. *Unbought & Unbossed.* 2nd Printed Edition. New York, NY: Houghton Miflin (T), 1970.
11. Lamb, Yvonne Shinhoster. *Pioneering Politician, Advocate Shirley Chisholm Dies.* January 24, 2005. http://www.washingtonpost.com/wp-dyn/articles/A46322-2005Jan4.html (accessed March 8, 2010).
12. Ibid.
13. Chisholm, Shirley. *Unbought & Unbossed.* 2nd Printed Edition. New York, NY: Houghton Miflin (T), 1970.

Chapter 4: Persist Against Opposition

1. Pickels, Dwayne E. *Joan of Arc.* New York, NY: Chelsea House Publishers, 2001.
2. Sanders, Anucha Browne, interview by Michel Martin. "Anucha Browne

Sanders Speaks Out on Knicks Case." *NPR News: Tell Me More.* (October 4, 2007).

3. Ibid.
4. NBC Sports via The Associated Press. "Jury Trial to Begin in Isiah Thomas Suit: Knicks president-coach accused of sexual harassment." *NBC Sports.* September 8, 2007. http://nbcsports.msnbc.com/id/20660004/ (accessed January 12, 2010).
5. Cornell, Kati. "Foul On Stephon: Knicks Star Slapped in MSG Sex Suit." *New York Post.* June 30, 2007. http://www.nypost.com/p/news/national/item_8ci27yGVwBwpQ4VFCF6lrK (accessed January 17, 2010).
6. Sanders, Anucha Browne, interview by Michel Martin. "Anucha Browne Sanders Speaks Out on Knicks Case." *NPR News: Tell Me More.* (October 4, 2007).
7. O'Keefe, Michael. "Q&A with legal expert on Anucha Browne Sanders case ." *New York Daily News.* September 15, 2007. http://www.nydailynews.com/sports/basketball/knicks/2007/09/15/2007-09-15_qa_with_legal_expert_on_anucha_browne_sa-1.html (accessed January 17, 2010).
8. NBC Sports. "Isiah Thomas Denies 'Repulsive Behavior': ' Knicks president, Hall of Famer denies sexual harassment accusations." *NBC Sports.* January 26, 2006.
9. Zambito, Thomas. "Anucha Browne Sanders settles suit." *New York Daily News.* December 11, 2007. http://www.nydailynews.com/news/2007/12/11/2007-12-11_anucha_browne_sanders_settles_suit-3.html.
10. ABC News/GMA. "The only way you make change is by being there; being silent never makes change, so speak up." *ABCNews.com.* October 3, 2007. http://abcnews.go.com/GMA/story?id=3682294&page=1 (accessed March 7, 2010).
11. Sanders, Anucha Browne, interview by Michel Martin. "Anucha Browne Sanders Speaks Out on Knicks Case." *NPR News: Tell Me More.* (October 4, 2007).
12. Ibid.
13. ABC News/GMA. "The only way you make change is by being there; being silent never makes change, so speak up." *ABCNews.com.* October 3, 2007. http://abcnews.go.com/GMA/story?id=3682294&page=1 (accessed March 7, 2010).
14. Steinem, Gloria. *Outrageous Acts and Everyday Rebellions.* New York, NY: Henry Holt & Co., 1984.
15. Ms. Magazine/Reuters. "Steinem Wants Clinton Censured, Not

Impeached." *Ms. Magazine.* September 29, 1998. http://www.msmagazine.com/news/uswirestory.asp?id=852.

16. Ibid.
17. Steinem, Gloria. " Women Are Never Front-Runners." *The New York Times*, January 8, 2008.
18. Fang, Jennifer. *Gloria Steinem: Pitting Race Against Gender.* January 9, 2008. http://www.racialicious.com/2008/01/09/gloria-steinem-pitting-race-against-gender/.
19. Ibid.
20. Ibid.
21. Steinem, Gloria. "Women Are Never Front-Runners." *The New York Times*, January 8, 2008.
22. Steinem, Gloria. *OpEd: Wrong woman, wrong message.* September 4, 2008. http://articles.laimescom/2008/sep/04/news/OE-STEINEM4(accessed July 12, 2010).
23. Brown, Heidi. "Equal Payback for Lilly Ledbetter." *Forbes.com.* April 28, 2009. http://www.forbes.com/2009/04/28/equal-pay-discrimination-forbes-woman-leadership-wages.html (accessed March 21, 2010).
24. Martin, Michel. "Lilly Ledbetter And The Fight For Gender Equality." *NPR News: Tell Me More.* February 11, 2009. http://www.npr.org/templates/story/story.php?storyId=100557186 (accessed April 17, 2010).
25. *LEDBETTER v. GOODYEAR TIRE & RUBBER CO., INC.* 550 U.S. 618 (2007) (The United State Supreme Court, May 29, 2007).
26. Ibid.
27. Ibid.
28. Obama, President Barack. "White House Blog: It's A Wonderful Day-REMARKS BY THE PRESIDENT UPON SIGNING THE LILLY LEDBETTER BILL." *Whitehouse.gov.* January 29, 2009. http://www.whitehouse.gov/blog_post/AWonderfulDay/ (accessed April 17, 2010).
29. Pickert, Kate. "2 Minute Bio: Lilly Ledbetter." *Time in Partnership with CNN.* January 29, 2009. http://www.time.com/time/nation/article/0,8599,1874954,00.html (accessed March 17, 2010).

Chapter 5: Speak Up For Justice

1. Asby, Ruth. *Rosa Parks: Freedom Rider.* New York, NY: Sterling Publishing Co, Inc., 2007.
2. Parks, Rosa. *Rosa Parks: My Story.* New York, NY: The Penguin Group, 1992.

3. Rosa Parks Facts. "The Mother of Civil Rights." *RosaParksFacts.com.* http://www.rosaparksfacts.com/rosa-parks-civil-rights-movement.php (accessed March 18, 2010).
4. Garrow, David J. *Bearing The Cross: Martin Luther King, Jr., and the Southern Christian Leadership Conference.* New York, NY: HarperCollins, 1986.
5. Linder, Doug. *Susan B. Anthony: A Biography.* 2001. http://law2.umkc.edu/faculty/projects/ftrials/anthony/sbabiog.html (accessed March 8, 2010).
6. Hill, Anita. *Speaking Truth to Power.* New York, NY: First Anchor Books, 1998.
7. Thomas, Clarence. "Hearing of the Senate Judiciary Committee on the Nomination of Clarence Thomas to the Supreme Court." Washington, DC, October 11, 1991.
8. Palmer, Barbara. "Ten years later, Anita Hill revisits the Clarence Thomas controversy." *Stanford University: Stanford Report.* April 3, 2002. http://news.stanford.edu/news/2002/april3/anitahill-43.html (accessed April 5, 2010).
9. Ibid.
10. Hill, Anita. *Speaking Truth to Power.* New York, NY: First Anchor Books, 1998.
11. Ibid.
12. Hill, Anita. "New York Times OP-ED: The Smear This Time." *The New York Times.* October 2, 2007. http://www.nytimes.com/2007/10/02/opinion/02hill.html (accessed May 21, 2010).
13. Palmer, Barbara. "Ten years later, Anita Hill revisits the Clarence Thomas controversy." *Stanford University: Stanford Report.* April 3, 2002. http://news.stanford.edu/news/2002/april3/anitahill-43.html (accessed April 5, 2010).
14. "Evita Peron Biography." *The Official Evita Peron Website.* April 1997. http://www.evitaperon.org/part1.htm (accessed March 5, 2010).
15. Ibid.
16. Ibid.
17. Ibid.
18. Ibid.
19. HistoryNet.com. "Seneca Falls Convention: First Women's Rights Convention." *HistoryNet: American History.* June 12, 2006. http://www.historynet.com/seneca-falls-convention-first-womens-rights-convention.htm/2 (accessed January 17, 2010).
20. Ibid.

21. Ibid.
22. Ibid.

Chapter 6: Insist on Integrity

1. Ackman, Dan. "The 'Warning' Of Kenneth Lay ." *Forbes.com.* January 15, 2002. http://www.forbes.com/2002/01/15/0115topnews.html (accessed December 12, 2009).
2. Time.com. "Viewpoint: Ken Lay Still Isn't Listening." *Time.com in partnership with CNN.* May 28, 2006. http://www.time.com/time/magazine/article/0,9171,1198927,00.html (accessed June 17, 2010).
3. Ibid.
4. Ibid.
5. Leung, Rebecca. "Meet A Major-League Whistleblower: Woman Who Exposed Mutual Fund Scandal Talks To 60 Minutes II." *CBS News.* July 7, 2004. http://www.cbsnews.com/stories/2004/02/17/60II/main600649.shtml (accessed January 15, 2010).
6. Investor Voice. "Wall Street's whistle-blower." *InvestorVoice.ca.* April 1, 2004. http://www.investorvoice.ca/PI/534A.htm.
7. Financial Women's Association. "FWA–NJ: NOREEN HARRINGTON AND THE ROLE OF THE WHISTLE-BLOWER." *Financial Women's Association.* September 10, 2010. http://www.fwa.org/event/2010_0930_nj_nharrington.pdf (accessed October 17, 2010).
8. Leung, Rebecca. "Meet A Major-League Whistleblower: Woman Who Exposed Mutual Fund Scandal Talks To 60 Minutes II." *CBS News.* July 7, 2004. http://www.cbsnews.com/stories/2004/02/17/60II/main600649.shtml (accessed January 15, 2010).
9. Dugas, Christine. "Spotlight hits whistle-blower." USA Today.com. December 9, 2003. http://www.usatoday.com/money/perfi/funds/2003-12-09-whistleblow_x.htm
10. Ripley, Amanda, and Maggie Sieger. "Coleen Rowley: The Special Agent." *Time In Partnership With CNN.* December 30, 2002. http://www.time.com/time/magazine/article/0,9171,1003988,00.html (accessed February 7, 2010).
11. Ibid.
12. Time.com. "The Bombshell Memo: Coleen Rowley's Memo to FBI Director Robert Mueller." *Time.* May 21, 2002. http://www.time.com/time/covers/1101020603/memo.html (accessed March 17, 2010).
13. Ripley, Amanda, and Maggie Sieger. "Coleen Rowley: The Special Agent."

Time In Partnership With CNN. December 30, 2002. http://www.time.com/time/magazine/article/0,9171,1003988,00.html (accessed February 7, 2010).

14. Ibid.
15. Ibid.
16. Turse, Nick. "Bush's War on Civil Servants: Marlene Braun." *Pacific Views*. May 28, 2005. http://www.pacificviews.org/weblog/archives/001686.html (accessed January 17, 2010).
17. Ibid.
18. Ibid.

Index

CPSIA information can be obtained at www.ICGtesting.com
261046BV00001B/1/P
9 781592 995813